Contents

Preface

The idea for this book began to evolve at a workshop on "Christianity and the Arts" organized by Walter Farquharson in 1991 when he was Moderator of the United Church of Canada. It could be argued that its genesis goes back to a conversation around a dining room table when Clair Woodbury's wife, Mary, suggested to Walter that he gather people together around the arts as part of his contribution as Moderator — but that is another story. Mary and Clair attended that workshop at Naramata Centre in British Columbia. It was a marvelous time with potters, song-writers, artists and painters sharing their insights and their work and Walter himself reading some of the poetry that has made him a much-appreciated hymn writer.

The question emerged: if arts like painting, poetry, literature, dance, drama and pottery can be ministries, could the activities we have tradition-ally considered to be ministry be approached as art? That was the challenge that Clair decided to take up himself and to share with Clark Saunders.

Between us, we bring to this enterprise a variety of experiences in congregational ministry. At the time of that Naramata workshop, Clair Woodbury was on staff at St. Stephen's College in Edmonton, Alberta. There he served as Director of a national program of research into the ways that new congregations develop and the things that make them thrive. Previously, he had served small and medium-sized congregations. Since completing the research program, he has become the Director of the Cana-dian Centre for Congregational Life, a group that conducts workshops and facilitates problem-solving in congregations across the whole ecumenical spectrum.

Clark Saunders has served rural, suburban and urban churches, and is currently on staff at Knox-Metropolitan United Church in Edmonton. His writings on liturgy, ministry and church history have been published in Britain and Canada. As a parish minister he tries to bring creativity to his own practice of ministry and supports others in the congregation as they express their creative gifts.

In writing about ministry as an art, we wanted to speak not only to those who practice ministry as a primary profession. As well, our intent was to say something to congregational members who are coming to see their service to the church and their work in the world as ministries. As Loren Mead of the Alban Institute reminds us in his groundbreaking books,[1,2] the central task of congregations today is to be "seminaries of the future," training people for the work of ministry.

Certainly, if you are serving a congregation as ministry personnel, ministering in a number of ways on any given day and spending considerable time training and supporting people in their ministries — this book was designed for you. And if you are one of those lay people who exercises a ministry of caring for a family, tries to think and act ethically amid the complex ambiguities of the modern workplace, visits weekly in a seniors' lodge, shares in the leadership of worship, teaches the young or leads a youth program — this book is for you, too.

In Part I of this meditation on ministry as an art, Clark Saunders shares his insights into conducting worship, preparing and preaching sermons, choosing music for worship and integrating it into services, administering sacraments and rites of passage, and providing pastoral care. He concludes with some thoughts about the leadership that staff members and boards can give their congregation. In examining all of these subjects, he goes in search of the qualities that we can bring to them that can make them art-forms.

Clair Woodbury's experience in congregational ministry and in cross-Canada research come into play in Part II as he examines what it means to make arts of innovation, management, facilitating in a conflict situation, and offering encouragement to one another. Out of sixteen years' experience in a university setting, Clair comments on the art of education. His thoughts on the art of giving are informed by his studies of giving patterns in new congregations. And you will hear a personal note as he explores two themes that are crucial in any ministry: loyalty to those who minister beside us, and staying in love with the God who is at the centre of it all.

That is what the book is about and how it came to be. You may choose to concentrate on the sections that apply to your own particular interests in ministry, or you can read the whole book because all our ministries depend on one another in the community of God's people. Whichever approach you take, we hope these chapters encourage you to see the potential for ministry to become a lively art — or, rather, a collection of lively arts — and a fertile field for the artistic expression of your relationship with God and your neighbour.

Clark Saunders
Clair Woodbury

Edmonton, Alberta
September 1996

1   Loren Mead, *The Once and Future Church* (Washington: Alban Institute, 1993).

2   _____, *Transforming Congregations for the Future* (Washington: Alban Institute, 1994).

Foreword

by Walter Farquharson

"To make an art of ministry means to be open to new and deeper insights into the nature of God and God's will for our times. It means being willing to incorporate those new understandings into our worship and our daily lives."

Coming to these words near the end of this book, I found myself pausing to wonder at the many ways in which Clark and Clair had combined the artistic spirit with passion, and tested techniques, to offer an exciting perspective on ministry within the church and our contemporary communities. I have found within this book that which is affirming. I also found that which was challenging and stretching of both imagination and of my familiar ways of doing things. I realized that in the reading I had become open to new and deeper insights into the nature of God and of God's will for our times. I had touched many understandings that would be incorporated into my living as a person of God's love and as a minister of that love. Clair and Clark, these two artists, these tested practitioners of the art of ministry, had worked their magic on me, and I had been bathed again in grace!

I was privileged through my years of growing up and my years of working in church and community to be encouraged and enabled by many who practiced their ministries as art. I found myself thinking of several of them as I read this book. One such person was a woman many of us called Grandma Cutler. She had been raised within a strict offshoot of frontier Ontario Methodism — and dancing in any form was prohibited. By the time I knew Grandma Cutler she was an older lady who had raised her family in Saskatchewan. She possessed an innate sense of rhythm and a love for good times. Over 70, as part of a family dance band, she was still playing piano Saturday nights for community dances. On summer Sunday mornings she often went with me to a little school house where I was conducting services of worship. I am not sure whether she was a full five feet tall or just short of it. I do remember that she had a way of swinging up onto the piano bench to play with passion and love the hymns of the church. She had resolved her inner conflict about dancing in this way, "I figure if the Good Lord hadn't wanted us to laugh we wouldn't have been created ticklish — and if we weren't supposed to dance we wouldn't have had feet that set to tapping whenever we heard good music." I loved her theology — and, more importantly, her deep and joyful faith.

The times in which we live are marked by many things, including an insidious fearfulness and defensiveness that is reflected in our economics, our politics and our daily conversations. It is highlighted in every news cast and talk show and it is amply demonstrated in the life of many congregations and denominational structures. We are much more likely to chant litanies of complaint than to sing anthems of celebration; to be aware of what is not available or possible for us than to see our own promise and potential.

This book will surprise you in many ways. It is hard to find within it one line of carping or complaint. It addresses the life we actually live now within communities of faith and within the society we are part of and does not succumb to any temptation to vilify or to whitewash. The authors manage to be faithful to our heritage without allowing that to fetter us. They point us towards the future with hopefulness and encourage appropriate risking for, and into, that future.

This is a book for all ministers — volunteer and professional — within the church. It enables us to look at the things we are doing and might be doing, to celebrate appropriately and to get on with a joyful service, seeking integrity and faithfulness in all things. It is profoundly visionary and immediately practical. The straightforwardness of vocabulary and style is disarming. Again and again the reader will stop to wonder at the depth that is being explored, and the breadth of knowledge and experience that is being drawn upon.

This book provides the church with a most timely resource — certainly it will serve as a source of renewal for those who pick up a copy and read it for their own purposes. But here is an ideal instrument to work through in any committees or boards of the church and here is an engaging source book for congregational, or other, retreats. As I read it, my list of those friends and co-workers with whom I would want to share it just continued to grow. My imagination danced with the possibilities of using this resource with people whose ministries I celebrate and who, I know, are looking for something that would free them to use the artistry that is theirs and to develop new ways to give expression to their work and ministries. Theological educators and leaders of training programs for ministers, professional and volunteer, will welcome this book and will encourage deep reflection on its content and context.

I remember well the conversation around the Woodbury's dining table that is referred to in the Preface of this book. I remember the joy and passion as we explored some possibilities — and I remember the richness of the gatherings that took place as the ideas generated around that and other tables took flesh in a series of programs held across Canada, from Newfoundland to the Naramata Centre in British Columbia. Such a variety of artists gathered to reflect on art and faith and to give expression to both within an encouraging and life-giving community! We called the events "Spirit Dancing" and together we celebrated the Spirit's dancing in and through creation, community and church — and in and through each of us.

I believe the authors' purpose will be again and again fulfilled as readers "see the potential for ministry to become a lively art — or, rather, a collection of lively arts — and a fertile field for the artistic expression of (their) relationship with God and (their) neighbour."

Spirit dancing on the waters,
give your people their new birth,
healing, loving one another
in community with earth.

Spirit dancing on the waters,
we would come and dance with you
'til our world is filled with music
and in Christ all things are new.[1]

Thank you, Clark and Clair, you have gifted us in the sharing of your artistry, and you have called to us in a most inviting and compelling way to be the artists we can become. Ministry as an *Art* offers each of us an exciting participation in the Spirit's dance within our time and within our ministries in our churches and communities. If we once start dancing, who knows when we'll stop!

The Very Reverend Walter H. Farquharson
Former Moderator of The United Church of Canada

---

1   from "Spirit Dancing," a hymn by Walter Farquharson and Lori Erhardt,
      used as a theme hymn at the Spirit Dancing gatherings and now published in
      Voices United: The Hymn and Worship Book of The United Church of Canada.

Foreword

by Keri K. Wehlander

There is a rabbinical story I heard once concerning the crossing of the Red Sea in which the waters did not part when Moses raised his staff over them. The story went on to say that the waters would only part when one of the Israelites was willing to take the first step in faith.

The way we approach an experience, a task or a relationship has a tremendous impact on what evolves. A first step taken with intent can make all the difference. In *Ministry as an Art*, Clair Woodbury and Clark Saunders invite us to take a fresh look at how we approach leadership and responsibility within the church and then encourage us to do so as artists.

Georgia O'Keeffe once wrote, "Nobody sees a flower — really — it is so small it takes time — we haven't time — and to see takes time..."[1] As a painter, she understood the discipline of paying attention. When Jesus taught, "Consider the lilies of the field, how they grow..." he was encouraging his followers to practice the very same discipline.

In roles of church leadership, many of us take on responsibility for a dizzying array of demands. In doing so, we can get so caught up in what needs to be done that we forget to look at the *how* and *why* of what we are doing. Paying attention to these areas of our work and leadership requires self-awareness, honesty and a desire to keep our relationship with God up to date. As Clark Saunders notes in his chapter on The Art of Leadership, "More and more writers are concluding that, of the factors that make for effective leadership, one that cannot be ignored is the interior life of the leader." The understanding of ministry as artistry implies that we recognize that our leadership requires much more than checking tasks off our "To Do" list. It challenges us to learn to see ourselves, the world we live in and the faith we profess more clearly and integrate these understandings more deeply into our living.

When we approach our work as art, we pay attention to the how and why of it. A creative approach also implies that we ask ourselves "*What if?*" and explore the ideas that come from asking such a question. This involves risk-taking and, no doubt, will evoke some fears. The rabbinical story of the Red Sea contrasts the one who risked in faith with those who held back in fear. Artistry in our work as church leaders means that we work from the foundation of grace, rather than cling to the pendulum of fear.

Ministry as an Art not only provides encouragement for an artistic approach to ministry, it presents specific, practical suggestions as well. I find that such suggestions often spark my own ability to ask myself "what if?" around my work and my particular context of ministry. For example, Clair Woodbury makes the following suggestion in his chapter on The Art of Social Action: "Another way to stimulate creativity is to push for three alternative scenarios for any given situation. My first idea is often what I want to happen and the second is what I think ought to happen. When I push for a third possibility I may just stumble on what God wants to happen." Suggestions such as these in the book might prove to be inventive discussion starters for committees or staff teams working within a church. Specific chapters, such as The Art of Pastoral Care, might be read by the members of a pastoral visitation team within a congregation as a way of seeing their ministry in a new light. Similarly, The Art of Managing Conflict might be quite helpful for a church council to discuss and reflect on as a way of bringing about new understandings and better communication.

There is a quality in those who do ministry as an art that is hard to define, but easy to recognize when we see it. Each of us has marvelled at individuals who have the ability to combine specific skills with a style all their own, which results in seemingly effortless moments of carrying out a task. For instance, a friend of mine is able to chair meetings with a combination of pastoral presence and attention to process that I find quite remarkable. Her ease and artistry make the meetings she chairs a pleasure to be a part of. The authors of this book speak of the importance of authenticity, technique and passion. I certainly see all three qualities present in my friend's ability. I also see a quality which Thomas Merton describes when he writes: "Art enables us to find ourselves and lose ourselves at the same time."[2]

Approaching ministry as an art, at its best, enables us to participate fully in God's grace, and in doing so, become living statements of that grace in the daily work that we do. May the suggestions and ideas in this book serve as an encouragement for us all to do just that.

Keri K. Wehlander, author
Joy is Our Banquet

1   Georgia O'Keeffe, "About Myself," *One Hundred Flowers* (New York: Knopf/Callaway, 1987)

2   Thomas Merton, *A Thomas Merton Reader*, ed. Thomas P. McDonnell (New York: Image Books, 1974), p. 387.

Part I

Clark Saunders

Introduction

My father was very sure about certain matters pertaining to the universe. To him all good things — trout as well as eternal salvation — come by grace and grace comes by art and art does not come easy.

— Norman Maclean, *A River Runs Through It*[1]

When I was a boy and took piano lessons, I sometimes played in the local music festival. Marks were awarded 50% for technique, and 50% for musicianship. An aspiring pianist could not afford to neglect either of these aspects of piano playing.

Technique is developed and improved by playing scales and chords and arpeggios and exercises to strengthen the muscles and increase agility. A pianist's abilities are limited without many hundreds of hours spent working on technique. But a pianist will not go far without developing a sense of artistry or musicianship. Some of this may be a natural gift — a sensitivity or an intuitive response to the message and the mood of the music — but some of it is acquired. When performing a created work, the pianist needs to show an understanding of the composition and a sense of empathy with the intention of the composer. Without technique, the most creative pianist will lack the discipline needed to bring off a creditable performance. Without musicianship, the pianist's efforts may produce considerable admiration for his or her skill, but it will be a performance that is lacking in soul, in inner life.

Those who practice Christian ministry cannot do their work without becoming competent in their performance of tasks. This book is based on the premise that ministry is not only a well-practised technique, but also an art.

There are a number of things that are true of artists in general and are also true of those who minister. An artist, for example, knows something of both medium and message. The medium may be oils or clay or words or dance or a musical instrument. Whatever it is, the artist must know the

3

medium and be friends with it. But the artist must also have a message, something to say. An artist needs to be able to help people to see or hear or feel something they might not otherwise experience. In other words, the artist brings a particular point of view, a particular perception of reality, a particular interpretation of the raw data of life, and uses a particular medium to express that point of view or perception or interpretation.

All of these things are true of those who practise the art of ministry. In fact, it could be said that, in approaching Christian ministry as art, we are taking our cue from the original artist whom we name as God. God, we believe, has a message for creation: a message of love and mercy, a call to justice and hope. And like human artists, God uses a variety of media to communicate this message. God's media could be said to include the works of creation itself as well as acts of providence and redemption. God communicates through the words of scripture and through the Word made flesh in Jesus Christ. And God-as-artist acts through the Holy Spirit at work in the lives of individuals and of communities. Not least, God-as-artist is active in our own creativity and imagination when we bring a sense of artistry to our life and work as Christian ministers.

That sense of artistry may not always be present in our practise of ministry. Speaking of just one aspect of ministry, William H. Willimon declares, "The preacher should have something to say." And, although he may overstate the case, Willimon still speaks to us when he goes on to claim, "One of the problems of mainline Protestantism is that we really don't have much interesting to say. Particularly we seem to lack something to say that can't be heard elsewhere. That's deadly. A lot of our people hear sermons as advice. It's usually interesting advice but the worst thing is that it's not any different advice than they could get at Rotary."[2]

Whether or not we agree with Willimon's assessment of current Protestant preaching, his statements seem to suggest that the minister-as-artist is someone who is passionate about communicating a particular perception of reality. Ministers as artists have something to say that they are convinced is important. This principle suggests a second aspect of the minister's artistry. A minister's art is profoundly connected to personhood. It is not something put on for the occasion. At a hospital bedside, the minister does not simply adopt a pastoral care mode, nor merely resort to the tricks of the trade in a counselling situation. Art is not to be confused with artifice. Those with whom we minister are better than we sometimes think at telling the difference.

If art is to be authentic, it will come from the authenticity of the artist. In ministry this is tricky. We have tried in recent decades to get away from the idea of ordered ministers and active lay people being seen as virtuous role models. For us to set ourselves up — or allow others to set us up — as paragons of virtue invites others to imagine the Christian life as a kind of perfection that is beyond their reach and that leaves them feeling judged as unworthy or inadequate. Paradoxically, it can also give people false comfort. They may be encouraged to believe that ministers are people who "have their act together," who have no doubts about matters of faith and doctrine and who live a very nearly blameless life. Both of these apparently contradictory reactions will give people a false notion of what it means to be a Christian.

And for the one who ministers, the role-model image can be a trap. Imperfections will become things that Christians feel they need to hide. They may even become things they need to hide from themselves. In that case, the kind of Christian faith and life that are modelled are those in which there is no room for growth or grace. It cannot be stressed too highly that those active in church life are just people, not paragons.

Discovering the art of ministry means finding a personal authenticity that is linked to God's grace. It may not mean modelling all the Christian virtues. But it does mean modelling a life through which something of God's grace — God's love and forgiveness and renewing power — can flow. This suggests that those for whom ministry is an art will see themselves as accepted by God, with all their incompleteness. By extension, the minister-as-artist — in sharing the need to learn, to be vulnerable, to be human — will invite others to experience something of this grace. At the same time, the minister will not give the impression that grace is cheap or that it is completely defined by God's passive acceptance of us "just as we are." "Grace," as Norman Maclean says, "comes by art and art does not come easy." One side of grace is God's acceptance of us and our having the grace to receive this acceptance. The other side of it is the way God empowers us to become more than we would otherwise be. God may accept us as we are, but God also will show us a still more excellent way.

The pursuit of excellence is a concept that has provoked a variety of reactions in the church. To some it smacks of an appeal to elitism and to misguided ambition. It may inspire an unhealthy "drivenness." It may lead to workaholism. It may encourage the very competitiveness that has become anathema to so many in the church. The idea of aspiring to excellence may suggest that God does not, in fact, accept us as we are.

And yet, surely God's grace is not merely accepting; it is also empowering. And for those who are engaged in ministry of any kind, God's grace is not content with technical expertise and professional competence, much less with what often amounts to just plain mediocrity. The minister's art is to be fed by a divine grace that inspires effort and encourages growth. One aspect of grace is a spur to growth and development. If this is an aspect that encourages competition, let us take care to be in competition with our former selves and not against others — like those athletes whose greatest satisfactions are found, not in beating others, but in improving their own "personal best."

What seems to be missing so often in the way in which ministry is performed is an element that is found in every influential artist's work; that is *passion*. Part of an artist's authenticity is found in the sense that s/he cares passionately about what s/he does.

People in "paid accountable ministries" are not merely hacks or hirelings, and should not see themselves as such. For thirty years or more, there has been a growing sense of clergy as "professionals." This emphasis has had many benefits. They have learned to stand up for themselves and to resist attempts to take advantage of them. They have learned something of the importance of things like continuing education, self-care, and the stewardship of their resources of time and energy.

The idea of the paid minister as professional was one whose time had come. As with other good things, it is possible to have too much of this one. Whatever we have gained from a sense of cool professionalism, it is no substitute for warm passion. Ministry is not merely a profession; it is also what it always has been: a vocation, a calling.

The volunteers in our churches who exercise an effective ministry teaching the young or visiting the sick tend to be the ones who have experienced an irresistible call to this work. Professional ministers who are also artists are persuaded that this is what they must do with their lives. They care passionately about the message that they feel God has given them to share.

Exploring the nature of ministry as art is an enterprise that has about it the feeling of taking a jellyfish for a walk on the end of an elastic band. Ministry as art is not easy to define or pin down. It is not the sort of thing that can be outlined succinctly in a "how to" manual for ministers, whether "ordered" or lay. That is partly because art is difficult to quantify or measure. We can't always see it. We may have difficulty defining it. And yet we can usually tell when it is present — and when it is missing.

In the chapters that follow we will be searching for that elusive quality of art in various aspects of Christian ministry. We will be trying to sharpen our ability to recognize a minister's art when we see it. And we will be working toward a clearer understanding of what the art of ministry really is.

1   Norman Maclean, *A River Runs Through It* (University of Chicago, 1976. Pocket Books edition, 1992), p. 5.

2   William H. Willimon, as quoted in "Believing 'this stuff is true'," *United Church Observer* (November, 1992), pp. 45-47.

Chapter 1

The Art of Worship

*To help us see to that part of our being that is not
dependent on wisdom. To our capacity for delight and wonder
and perhaps a glimpse of truth.*

— Joseph Conrad, quoted on the Greta Dale Mural in
the Centennial Concert Hall, Winnipeg, Manitoba

When we think of the arenas in which lay and "ordered" Christians
offer conspicuous leadership as artists, the first setting that comes to mind is
in the church on Sunday morning. Whatever other activities church members may be involved in, the one that brings most of us together on a regular
basis is congregational worship.

When you think of the Sunday service, what particular aspects of it have
the most significance for you? My hunch is that your answer included the
music or the sermon or both. In fact, art plays such an important part in our
approach to these two ingredients in the worship experience that we have
devoted a separate chapter to each of them. In this opening chapter we want
to think about the worship service as a whole and explore some of the things
that can make worship "art." We'll conclude by looking at how an artistic
approach can affect the way we deal with some specific elements in worship.

General Principles: Theory

The inscription on the large mural in the foyer of the Centennial
Concert Hall in Winnipeg seems appropriate for a space in which performing artists — symphony orchestras, dance and opera companies, recitalists,
and so on — "do their thing." But these words of dedication also have
overtones that sound not out of place in Christian worship. They articulate
a goal — a goal to engage aspects of our humanity that we may not be

conscious of every day. Like performance arts, worship is an activity that uses particular media to mediate between ideas and people. Those who design worship, like other artists, need to think about what it is they want to communicate to the people in the seats, what experience they want them to have, what part of their being they would like to touch, what realization or transformation they hope will take place so that, by the end of this activity, people will not be merely an hour older.

Generally speaking, what is it that we want a worship service to convey? This is a worthwhile question to ask because we will not know how to do something unless we know first what it is we want to do. Let me suggest that we intend the service to mediate something of God's grace, some aspect of the love and the hope God has for us, so that we can be empowered to respond with praise and commitment. If we can accept that working definition of the purpose of worship, it may be fair to ask whether those of us who plan and lead worship — whether Sunday by Sunday or on the odd occasion — really set out to accomplish that. Do we conduct worship in a way that is grace-full?

If that question sounds too vague and general, let's be more specific. Do we conduct worship in a way that has a sense of significance or of "occasion" about it? Do we approach it — and encourage others to approach it — with a sense of expectancy? Is there a feeling of immediacy about it for us that will rub off on those who share the experience with us?

Years ago I heard about a minister beginning a service with a call to worship that was meant to sound trendy. In a world-weary voice, the worship-leader intoned, "Well, here we are again, Lord." The air was not exactly promise-crammed! The congregation was not being encouraged to expect anything very exciting or helpful to happen. How much better to begin in a way that raises people's expectations that something significant is about to take place.

Our attitude to worship will speak of the artist in us if we approach it with a sense of occasion, with a respect for those who worship with us and for the importance of what we are doing. In an effort not to seem stuffy or overly formal, some of us lead worship in a way that is slipshod and casual and uninspiring. Queen Victoria is supposed to have complained that Mr. Gladstone — unlike the charming Disraeli — addressed her as if she were a public meeting. Worship is sometimes conducted as if it were merely a public meeting and not a gathering of God's people for a sacred purpose.

What this means is that, as artists, we will strive for excellence when we prepare and lead in worship. This is an activity that is worthy of the best we have to give. It should be conducted in a way that inspires confidence because it is clear that we have prepared carefully and thoughtfully. Of course, this doesn't mean that we should be perfectionists in an uptight sense, unwilling to forgive ourselves for our mistakes. We need to leave room both for our own humanity and for the work of the Spirit. Worship may include unanticipated glitches. But it is also true — as true of worship services as of concert performances — that sometimes the most magical moments are the unexpected and serendipitous ones. (An unscripted but apt comment from a child in the Children's Time, for instance, can be a genuine moment of truth.) If worship's basic purpose is to mediate grace, then as worship leaders we need to accept these moments graciously and let them be.

If you are beginning to sense something of the awesomeness of conducting worship, your burden may not be lightened by a reminder that there is a sense of responsibility — and even of accountability — about it. Worship, like music, is in the nature of a re-created art. Music is created once by the composer. Then it is re-created every time it is performed. Each performer brings something unique to the performance — something of that unique emotion and thought and experience. As well, most performers take seriously their responsibility to try to understand the intention of the composer, to be faithful to the composer's purpose, to be consistent with the composer's style, as they develop their own interpretation of a particular work.

This same sense of responsibility is important for worship leaders. Just as each of us brings particular gifts of personality and experience to bear on the theme of a service, we recognize that that theme is not plucked out of thin air. It is suggested to us by the scripture readings for the day and by the particular faith tradition in which we stand. These are things that have authority for us. As artists, we may bring our own convictions and understanding to this raw material. We may hope as well to offer fresh perspectives and new insights as our particular artistic expression. In some cases, we may even want to critique certain aspects of our faith tradition or propose a radical reinterpretation of a portion of scripture. The one thing we are *not* free to do is to ignore the texts and the creations of those who have gone before us, just as a concert pianist is not free to ignore the notes on the page.

We can, however, be like a jazz pianist who, while having a basic theme to work from, is not only free but is *expected* to improvise in a way that adds to the interpretation and speaks to the audience in a fresh way. Or we can be like a Bel Canto singer who embellishes the written music by "gracing" some of the notes. Whatever interpretation a musician gives to the music, the printed text and the traditions that surround it remain a constant reference point that must be recognized. This is no less true for those who practise the art of worship.

Now all these parallels between the performing arts and the leadership of worship may be making you feel a little uneasy. People who teach courses on worship are often at pains to point out that worship is not a performance. I have attended more than one Worship Committee meeting where the main item on the agenda was the issue of whether or not applause should be discouraged in our worship services. The argument of those who were opposed to our applauding children's groups when they performed in church was just *that* — that it encouraged them to see their offering as a perform-ance and worship as a concert, a form of entertainment.

I am less convinced by that argument than I used to be and less nervous about drawing comparisons between performances and worship. I remember a rabbi once dealing with the concern that people in the pews saw the people "up there at the front" as putting on a show for their benefit. "There is a sense in which worship *is* putting on a 'show'," he said. "But it isn't a case of some of us putting on a show for the others; we're *all* putting on a show for God. And we hope God will be pleased."

The concern that the rabbi was addressing is the one that sees the performance model as encouraging the people in the pews to be merely passive observers of the show that is being put on — as if worship were a spectator sport. It encourages a lack of involvement. And yet, haven't most of us attended a play that has involved us and the rest of the audience more surely than some of the worship services we've sat through? Our participa-tion may not have been expressed in any formal way, by standing to sing or by reading aloud words printed in a program, but it may have shown in our body language by sitting on the edge of our seats, or in our laughter or our tears. If we artists who design worship services could touch people in that way and could elicit such a participative response, wouldn't we be grateful?

I once attended a service at Glide Memorial United Methodist Church in downtown San Francisco. My first reaction, and with a note of disap-proval, was that this was like a performance. Aside from a few simple choruses, the congregation did no singing. The music — and there was a lot of it — was performed almost entirely by a Gospel-style choir. Everything was applauded. The sermon even got a standing ovation! As the service developed, I began to realize that this congregation was anything *but* passive and uninvolved. Their applause was an important part of their participation, a culturally acceptable way of identifying with what was happening, of saying, "Amen!" Although they sang very little, repeatedly they would stand and clap rhythmically as the choir sang, or sway in time to the music. A sign on the video camera platform warned, "Please do not bang or pound on this platform while the camera is operating." Clearly this was a place where participation was expected!

Of course, one of our concerns about the performance model — and a legitimate one — is that it can lend itself to glorifying the performer. While it is good for us, as Christian communities, to affirm the gifts of those in our midst, we need to be cautious about giving more attention and praise to the gifts that receive public exposure in worship than we do to those that are exercised quietly, behind the scenes. Most important, the thing that makes worship most different from the play at the repertory theatre is that worshippers see God as the primary participant — the initiator, in fact — of the activity in which we participate.

We've said something about the message that worship is meant to convey — some specific aspect of the larger message of the grace of God revealed in Jesus Christ and witnessed to in scripture. And we've said something about the medium through which that message is conveyed — the medium of worship. We've suggested that both the medium and the message need to be treated with respect. But so does the audience — in this case, the congregation. As we'll see particularly in exploring the art of preaching, it is important to take the congregation seriously and to begin where they are rather than where we imagine they are or think they ought to be. A generation ago we heard worship regularly criticized for not being relevant. Whatever the term may have meant then, today it suggests not only our need to be attuned to social realities, but to have our thumb on the pulse of the people who come to worship, to develop the message in a way that speaks to the realities of their lives, through media that they can understand.

This means more than seeing the congregation as a collection of unconnected individuals. Another way in which worship resembles a concert is that both are *corporate* activities. When people come together as a gathered community, things can happen that remind us that, in worship, we are more than the sum of our parts. Many people, when they are honest, will list "seeing my friends" as one of their main reasons for going to church. That fact should alert us to the realization that church members see Sunday morning as a social time. This is a fact that shouldn't be resisted. Worship leaders who are artists see it as a resource when they design the event that is to take place in what is so obviously a *social* context.

General Principles: Practice

If it is true that a gathering of individuals becomes more than the sum of its parts, it is no less true that a worship service is more than the sum of the items listed in the Sunday bulletin. The individual items certainly deserve attention — as you will see at the end of this chapter — but it is important not to see them as items on a shopping list. When you buy groceries, it may not matter in what order you pick things up, but part of the art of designing a worship service is in seeing that it is an event that has shape. One item needs to lead naturally to the next. It is necessary to have some input before you can expect a response. If, as an artist, you have an idea of where you would like people to be by the end of the service, you will have taken the first step in figuring out how to help them get there.

Practical considerations are important, of course. There is no point in planning to do something involving the children after they have left for Sunday school. Nevertheless, saying to yourself, "I think I'll put in my favourite hymn there because people will have been sitting for a while," does not speak of an artist's approach — especially if your favourite hymn has nothing to do with the theme of the service.

From the artist's perspective, there is a need for the elements in a worship service to come together in a satisfying whole and for the person responsible for coordinating the service to communicate with other leaders in a way that brings about that result. There is a need for coherence. There should be a feeling of integrity in the sense that the various parts of the service should be as well integrated as possible, not just dropped into the service without any connection to anything else.

Coherence and integrity do not imply homogeneity. By that I mean, for example, that we don't need to feel slavishly tied to the lectionary in choosing every hymn or writing every prayer. Sometimes it may not be possible to find an anthem that specifically reinforces one of the scripture texts; music that simply reflects the season of the Christian year is no less appropriate. At other times, a day of the year that deserves attention — Palm Sunday, for example — may also be the day for confirmation in your congregation, and you will need to say something about each of these themes. In any case, a service that has no variation in it or in which every ingredient from beginning to end harps on the very same theme can lack the kind of shape an act of worship needs. And it can leave people feeling the theme has been hammered to death.

The notion that worship is more than the sum of the parts listed in the order of service also suggests that continuity is important. It may be dangerous for us to get overly hung up about the details of "running" a service. On the other hand, church musician Linda Clark, in questioning church-goers, uncovered their concerns about the adverse effect of chaotic leadership.[1] If worship is meant to mediate grace, those little items of continuity need to be thought about and taken care of so they don't get in the way or distract people from the essential message.

Ask yourself: What happened when the offering was collected last time I was in church? Who announced it and how? Where were the offering plates prior to the announcement? Did the congregation stand when the offering was presented? Did they sing something? If so, what? What else happened as part of the presentation? What was done with the plates afterwards?

If you had trouble answering some of these questions, chances are that the offering was done well — so well that the mechanics did not draw attention to themselves. That is what a lay group at our church discovered when they sat down to prepare to lead in worship. They were amazed to find how many little details — bits of continuity in getting from one thing to another, in introducing a scripture reading, in closing off a sermon, in inviting people to pray — were things they had hardly noticed and were uncertain how to do; but they would have noticed them if they weren't there or were done awkwardly.

I have a brother who is a lighting designer in the theatre. He is both an artist and a technician. It used to bother him that theatre critics hardly ever mention his lighting in their reviews of theatrical performances — and after all the trouble he would go to. But gradually he consoled himself with the thought that lighting is most often noticed when it is badly done. When it contributes to the overall artistic impression it does not draw attention to itself. Its presence is too subtle to be noticed for its own sake. It is then that it proves the truth of the saying that "art conceals art."

By the same token, those of us who lead worship need to anticipate our needs as carefully as any stage manager. To find that the book we plan to read from is on the other side of the chancel, to stumble over some words because we hadn't read the text carefully beforehand, to ask, "What is the name of this child?" and discover that the font is empty — these things may not mean the end of the world but they do convey the message that we haven't honoured the activity of worship or the people whose worship we are leading sufficiently to prepare for it in an appropriate way.

Of course, even the most diligent planner can slip up occasionally. When your worst nightmare comes true and you can't for the life of you think what comes after "Our Father, who art in heaven," it is usually possible to meet the moment with grace — if only by "faking" it. I remember a great preacher once reading the scripture lesson for his sermon. He broke off in mid-sentence and said, "Oh, I'm sorry, I read further than I meant to." How much more graceful — and how much more of an artist — he would have been to find an appropriate place to stop without alerting the congregation to his mistake. In that case it might have been the content of the reading — rather than the fact that he had goofed — that would have stayed in their minds.

Media and the Senses

If we have identified worship as a medium for the message of God's grace, our thoughts about the practical considerations of worship would not be complete without some comments about the specific media that worship can use. It is often said that Christian worship — and Protestant worship especially — appeals almost entirely to one sense only: our hearing. We are big on words and music; these are things that are heard. It is easy to overstate the case, of course. Our eyes may give us more clues as to what is going on in the service than we realize. Nevertheless, we do have five senses, and those who see worship as art will want to appeal to all of them.

Worship is often spoken of in terms of words and action. Actions, of course, are seen and in worship, actions can be signs of grace. Whether we are thinking of a gracious gesture that invites the congregation to pray, or the symbolic action of breaking bread or pouring water or wine, the things we *do* (as well as the things we say) and the way we do them can convey something of God's grace.

Of course, our vision enables us to see not only symbolic movement, but symbols that are part of the setting of worship: crosses, pictures, banners, stained-glass windows. The ways the space itself is arranged can speak to us and convey something of worship's message. Some of these things may appear exactly the same week after week. Others can be moved or adapted in a way that brings us a new perspective.

Beyond hearing and sight, we have the senses of touch, taste and smell. We may not use our tactile sense in many different ways in worship, but worship leaders can include opportunities for people to greet one another with a handshake or a hug. Many people who come to worship crave human contact and find it reassuring. It can also help worshippers to feel more related to one another and enhance the corporate nature of the service. However, not all of us have the same personal touch boundaries and no one should be placed in a position where they cannot graciously decline a hug or a handshake. Similarly, if you are going to conduct a footwashing in a church where this practice is not a well-established tradition, you might want to offer this rite in a way that allows people the option of not participating if they do not feel comfortable with it.

Taste is a sense that responds to the elements that are served at Communion. How else do we use the medium of taste in worship? I once designed a service that allowed people to experience the four essential tastes — sweet, sour, salt, bitter — and related each to a passage of scripture. There is something enlivening about engaging a sense that we rarely think of in the context of worship.

The sense of smell is something that we may associate only with those traditions that use incense in worship. I recall a Maundy Thursday service when we anointed one another with perfumed oil and so called to mind the action of Mary of Bethany prior to Christ's crucifixion. However, again opting out must be allowed for. We discovered that the perfumed oil triggered some people's allergies, and they had to steer clear of it.

The use of imagination is the artist's stock in trade, and exciting things can happen when we exercise our imaginations on the senses. Of course, the audience always needs to be considered. It may be best, in trying out a new medium, to avoid services where people would naturally come expecting something conventional. It is important to take their feelings and sensitivities into account.

Thoughtful preparation for new experiences is important. I recall a service where we dramatized the renewal of baptismal vows by dipping evergreen boughs in water and sprinkling the congregation with it. In some ways it was an effective symbol, but people who were unprepared for it were visibly startled! And it is important to try to anticipate difficulties. Used with care, it is possible to expand the repertoire of media that we can use to convey the themes of worship.

Specifics

We conclude this chapter with some questions, hints and suggestions about the specific elements in worship, apart from music, the sermon, sacraments and "occasional" services. For the sake of convenience, let's take these items in order, based on the familiar reformation "Approach-Word-Response" pattern.

The Approach

Services often begin with a call to worship or a choral introit. Whether or not the text is scriptural, does it give a sense of occasion and a hint of things to come? Does it raise expectations? If the words are responsive, do the sentences given to the congregation sound natural on their lips? In the same way, the prayer of approach should be linked to the act of worship and the theme of this particular service. Does it connect people to God in this particular place and time?

Prayers of confession (which occur after the "Word" in most Anglican and Roman Catholic churches) can be very problematic. Often they are either too general or too specific. Does the prayer of confession acknowledge not only the bad in us that we try to deny, but the good in us that we sometimes fail to claim? Instead of a steady diet of self-condemnation, services at one church sometimes use a "prayer of affirmation" in which we rejoice in our identity as God's beloved creations. That may be no less worth declaring at the beginning of worship than our need for God's forgiveness.

The Word of God

The "Word of God" portion of the service is usually centred on the scripture readings and the sermon that is based on them. Whether or not the readings are taken from the lectionary, there is usually some theme or motif to bind them together. It may be helpful to introduce them — either as a group or individually — in order to draw out these themes. It is easy for us to let our minds wander when scripture is read unless we are encouraged to listen for something in particular. Leaders can help this to happen by introducing the readings, by choosing a translation that is easy to follow and that reflects values like inclusive language, and by the way they read. The text itself may be prescribed for us, but there is still an art to reading scripture effectively. (In one congregation I know, people who are interested in serving as lay readers receive training periodically from a member of the congregation who is experienced in public speaking.) Occasionally we can be creative in other ways, for example, in having a reading dramatized.

Churches that have a regular "Children's Time" or "Theme Conversation" usually include it in this part of the service. Conversations with children are not always easy. In fact, many preachers look on these few moments with greater fear and trembling than they do the sermon. The interchange of conversation with children is usually unscripted, spontaneous and — for those of us who have an above-average need for control in our lives — more free-wheeling than our comfort level may demand. The dangers and pitfalls are many: open-ended questions that may take us away off the track, or closed ones for which we have just one right answer in mind — and we will not give up until we get it; the temptation to play to the gallery and use the children for entertainment purposes, receiving as "cute" or "funny" a comment that a child may have made in all seriousness; the challenge of using language that is accessible to the younger ones without insulting the intelligence of the older ones; the list is endless. To strike just the right balance between ease and control requires art as well as skill. And as any Sunday school teacher knows, no less important than the point you are trying to get across is the relationship you are establishing with the children. In fact, the crucial thing about these weekly encounters is that they be done with grace. Much of the message is in the manner in which we engage the children.

The Response

The move to the "Approach-Word-Response" pattern in most of our Protestant churches a generation ago did something good for the Offering. By making it part of our response to the Word, it made it more difficult to think of the Offering as "the Collection" and to regard it as an interruption in the flow of the service, a kind of "word from our sponsor." Making an art of the Offering means seeing its symbolic value as an offering of all that we have and are in response to the proclamation of God's grace. Do the words we say and the actions we perform around the Offering help to do that? Are the offering plates actually presented, or do the ushers make a bee-line for the office so they can get a head-start on counting it?

And what about the announcements? It may be appropriate to include them as part of our response to the Word rather than seeing them as an impediment to the flow of the service. But, if they are included within the service, it will be necessary to work at helping people see the connection between the worship and the life and work of the congregation. An alternative is to deal with announcements before the service formally begins, as part of a gathering or community time.

The main prayers of the day — whether they are called the Pastoral Prayer, Prayers of Thanksgiving and Intercession, or Prayers of the People — are most likely to be both composed and led by someone in the congregation. There is opportunity here for creative thought in composing the prayers. Again, there needs to be both something we want to say and a sensitivity to the needs of the congregation. This prayer is corporate, after all, and not private. There is an opportunity to take people's gratitude and concerns and express them in ways that touch them because they feel heard.

I remember once, as a university student, attending a service led by Dr. David Hay, a professor at Knox College in Toronto and sometime moderator of the Presbyterian Church. It was exam time, and Dr. Hay included in his prayers the concerns of students. He phrased his petition in a way that suggested to me that, as a student, I was engaged in a noble enterprise and that someone was participating imaginatively in my concerns at that moment and thought they were worth praying about. I experienced that prayer as a work of art.

Of course, as with other elements in the service, there are dangers in public prayer. It is so easy for us to misuse prayer as an opportunity to preach. This is a hazard that can befall both the preacher who sees the prayers as one last chance to get the point across and the lay person who may never have a chance to preach and sees the prayer as an opportunity to include all his hobby horses. If words like "should" and "ought" are risky in sermons, it might be best to avoid them entirely in prayers!

Worship in many Protestant churches usually concludes with a Commissioning in which we are sent out into the world and a Blessing in which we are assured of God's continuing presence with us. Again these words may be taken from scripture, or they can be our own inventions. Either way, there is an art to choosing the right words, to making this moment a summing up without using it to compensate for our lack of clarity in the sermon, to saying enough without saying so much that the congregation's patience and interest diminish with each additional phrase.

Conclusion

Both the total experience of worship and the individual elements within the service can be enhanced when we approach them as "art." We have still to look at some of the most significant aspects of worship: preaching, music, and the sacraments and other rites. These form the subjects of the next three chapters.

1   Linda J. Clark, *Music in Churches* (Washington: Alban Institute, 1994), p. 22.

Chapter 2

The Art of Preaching

*Preaching is an art. For that reason it can never be reduced
to the mastery of certain techniques which automatically produce
good sermons. Though there are certain skills to be learned,
preaching is not a matter of technique but of being. Preaching
must come from the depths of the people who have been given an
irresistible divine call to speak the word of the Lord. If I am
tempted to be silent, confessed Jeremiah, "then within me there is
something like a burning fire shut up in my bones; I am weary
with holding it in, and I cannot" (Jeremiah 30:9).*

— Jay Weener, *Reformed Review*[1]

It isn't easy to define the ways in which preaching becomes a highly developed craft or an art, but some of the differences may be found in the preacher's approach to his or her work. The preacher who has developed the "skills" and "technique" that Jay Weener talks about may produce eloquent sermons, but it takes something more for a sermon to carry the kind of power we associate with art. Among other things, it takes "the need to preach," that feeling that Jeremiah talked about and that Paul sensed when he declared, "Woe to me if I do not proclaim the gospel!" (I Corinthians 9:16)

Of course, the artist's tools should not be neglected or despised. The preacher's primary medium is words. Kenneth Clark, the art historian, said, "just as I would look with suspicion on an artist who took no interest in his tools, so I find myself out of sympathy with the writer who is not interested in the sounds and overtones of words and in the rhythm of a sentence."[2] This caution applies particularly to preachers, because preachers do not merely write words; they also speak them. The words themselves may be a tool, but so is the human voice. Both words and voice deserve some attention.

The English writer, Thomas deQuincey, once made a famous distinction between what he called words of knowledge and words of power. No doubt the Bible contains some of each, but it is the words of power that grab us and hold us. When I was a boy in Sunday school, I was given a copy of the Gospel of John in the King James Version. I remember reading over and over those impressive opening words: "In the beginning was the Word, and the Word was with God, and the Word was God. The same was in the beginning with God ..." and so on. I wasn't at all sure that I knew what it meant, but I was in no doubt that here was something of great significance and power. The sounds and overtones gave me a sense of divine presence in the words.

In our culture, most preachers embark on their task after years of attending university and learning to think critically and to write analytically. Unfortunately, our essay-writing techniques often carry over into our sermon-writing. We create our sermons not as works of art but as academic treatises. We use words in a way that saps the power from them. We take things apart and make sense of them and sometimes leave them as powerless as a dissected poem.

Taking apart an internal combustion engine can be an enlightening experience. It can teach you how a car works, but when the exercise is over you can be left with nothing more than a pile of metal on the floor. A lot of sermons are like that. They take things apart in a way that helps our understanding but takes the power out of them.

It is also possible for a sermon to take the power out of people. Many of us have "sat under" preachers who have told us how bad we were, leaving us feeling responsible for all of society's ills, though powerless to do anything about the situation. Some of these preachers may look and sound like they are preaching with power — they may shout and wave their arms around — but their sermons are really draining the energy from the room and from the people in it.

Releasing the Power

How can preachers use words in ways that release power in people? Preaching should always begin with a text from scripture. When you develop the ability to release the power in passages from the Bible, your preaching takes on power. When you share with people how they can do this for themselves, you truly empower them.

It is tempting, immediately after reading over a passage for next Sunday's service, to get out the Bible commentaries to find out something about the context of the passage and about what some of the experts think it means. (After all, many of us were taught that the three most important things about interpreting the Bible are context, context and context.) To do that is to move immediately to that analytical mode that can take the power out of things. How much better to leave the text alone and let it speak for itself for a while.

Getting into a rhythm of sermon preparation is something that can help not only the preacher's craft, but his or her art as well. Read over the passages for the following Sunday early in the week and let them sit for a day or two. Jot down ideas that come to you. Many of these ideas will come out of your own experience. In fact, you may find that some verses in the readings jump out at you and speak with power to something within you. They may act as magnets for memories and ideas. If you are the sort of person who learns best in conversation, talk over your ideas with others — perhaps in a lectionary-based study group — and see whether that helps them to take shape. Some phases of sermon preparation are necessarily solitary and even lonely, but they don't all have to be.

Wait a while before checking the commentaries and adding the insights they bring. With this added background you may find that some of your ideas are not really in line with what the scripture writer was saying and have to be discarded. Other ideas will be brought into sharper focus and will give you something to work on. Give the passage a chance to germinate and interact with your life experience and there will be a better chance that the sermon will be your message and not somebody else's. In other words, there will be a better chance of the sermon being not merely clever communication but art as well.

Most of us who preach either regularly or occasionally have had the experience of wishing we could preach like someone else. We hear a church leader like former United Church of Canada moderator Lois Wilson or James Forbes of Riverside Church in New York City and wish we could preach like that. (Some of us have even wished we could preach with a Scottish or southern American accent so that the sound of our voices could compensate for the banality of what we have to say!) More than a few of us have gone so far — consciously or unconsciously — as to try to imitate other preachers. The problem is that, while imitation may be the highest form of flattery, it is not authentic. No one else has had the same life experience as you have. No one else will read the same passage of scripture and be touched by it in quite the same way as you. And if you are a preacher — while there is a universality to the gospel — no one has the gift to preach it in quite the same way as you have. The art of preaching will be elusive if you try to imitate someone else. If there is something distinctive in the content and style of your preaching, in your message and in the way you communicate it, you may find that it has a touch of art about it.

The Authority of Stories

What we are saying is that preaching as art must have something personal about it. A few generations ago, people who were learning to preach were cautioned against using personal references in their sermons. Using a story or illustration from your own experience was considered tacky and in poor taste. It was against the rules. The rules could be broken occasionally, but only if you prefaced your story with a phrase like, "If I may be allowed to make a personal reference...."

Nowadays that old taboo has disappeared. We have always known that what people remember from sermons is the illustrations. That is because most people think in pictures rather than in concepts. Jesus knew that. That is why he spoke about a woman pleading with a judge, and a man going down from Jerusalem to Jericho when he fell among thieves, and a shepherd leaving ninety-nine sheep to look for the one that was lost. These are images that stuck in the minds of his listeners for several decades before anyone thought to write them down.

Although memorable sermons have always been dotted with stories, these stories have often been used only to illustrate a point — a point that was frequently explained and developed at great length. Today, however, more and more preachers have been realizing that the real "meat" of the sermon is in the stories: so there should be more story and less analysis. Stories carry a power of their own and usually do not need to be explained or analyzed. When we find one of Jesus' stories explained in the Bible — like the story of the sower and the seed, for example — we can usually assume that the explanation is the work of someone in the early church who wanted to make sure the readers got the point; in other words, someone knew the story had power and didn't want to take a chance on the power escaping his control. Jesus himself was more trusting than that; when the story was told, those who had ears to hear would hear.

Stories — like paintings and other works of art — have the advantage of being able to engage people at different levels. One person may hear a certain message or moral in a story. The next person may pick up on a detail that touches his/her experience in a different way — just as two people looking at a cloud may see something different in it. The same story may challenge someone intellectually and elicit from someone else a deep emotional response. That is part of a story's unchained power. Those of us who like to tell people what a story means may have a hard time resisting the urge to spell it out for people, but a story is a delicate thing, so we must resist that urge or we may kill it.

I have had the experience of ending a sermon with a powerful story and having to struggle against the temptation to add just one more paragraph to sum it all up. I have also had the experience of leaving the sermon open-ended and finding an interesting response from the congregation. Some have been uncomfortable and have actually asked, "What did you mean by that?" Others have appreciated the chance to take away something that is incomplete — something they can continue to ponder and work on. They seem to have understood the principle that art leaves room for a response.

Stories have a life of their own. That can make them risky, but that is also what can make them powerful. Preaching that uses stories effectively can be both risky and powerful.

Now, we began this section by saying that preaching as art must have something personal about it. Stories are personal. Some of the stories we tell in sermons may be second-hand. We have read or heard them somewhere, and they have spoken to us. Others may involve ourselves or people we know. Whether first-hand or second-hand, a story that in some way has touched us has a good chance of touching others. Sharing that story is a way of sharing ourselves, of making the sermon personal, of helping the word to take on flesh, of making the sermon art.

Telling a story can make us seem vulnerable — especially if it is a story involving ourselves. That perhaps is why earlier generations avoided telling personal stories. Preachers were supposed to be strong and secure — people who had found the answers to all the questions about faith and life. If preaching was to be authoritative, people thought it should not reveal too much about the preacher. That would be too human. And when people appear too human, it's hard to keep them on a pedestal.

Now, it seems, many of us are more inclined to trust a preacher who is willing to reveal some doubts and questions as well as faith and convictions, a preacher who is willing to share moments of struggle and searching as well as moments of triumph and discovery, times not only of ministering but of having received ministry. In fact, that kind of preaching has about it a kind of authority that impersonal preaching lacks. There is something authentic and concrete about a preacher who speaks out of experience and shares things that have touched him/her personally. That message has a degree of reality and a touch of art about it.

Of course, there are cautions that need to be kept in mind if we are to be more personal in our preaching. For one thing, there is the danger of betraying confidences. This may be another reason why our predecessors were reluctant to tell personal stories. To tell a story that involves other people — and especially people known to the congregation — is a contravention of professional ethics. It is essential that we get permission from the people who appear in our stories — even if the person's identity is disguised — before sharing their experience with others.

Then there is the question of where self-disclosure crosses a line and becomes self-indulgence. A minister who was going through a painful separation and divorce managed to bring his own feelings and experiences into every sermon he preached for many weeks in a row. Finally, a member of his congregation took him aside and said, "John, you're going to have to stop bleeding all over us every Sunday." There may be a therapeutic aspect to preaching, but preaching is not therapy. A preacher who does not make that distinction is valuing his/her own words more highly than the Word and placing his/her own needs ahead of those of the congregation.

The Artist's Audience

Perhaps it's time to say something more about the role of that congregation — the listeners — in the sermon. Preaching, like all art, is a form of communication. There is a message that is transmitted from the artist to the audience. Those who preach know how difficult their task can be when there appears to be no spark of interest on the part of a congregation that seems to be actively engaged in counting the tiles in the ceiling or gazing out the window. Many can attest, as well, to the energy they receive from a congregation that appears to be eager and attentive. That's when preaching truly becomes a corporate enterprise.

A young ordinand on his first charge was preaching a sermon to a sparse congregation. It was heavy sledding, and he was feeling not very encouraged. At one point, he made a statement and followed it up with the rhetorical question, "Now, isn't that true?" And a woman in the congregation, her eyes coming to life, nodded vigorously. For the preacher that was the turning point in the sermon. It was a gesture that told him he was no longer alone. The rest of the sermon was preached with a passion that, until that moment, had been missing.

There are artists, of course, who care little or nothing for their audiences. There are painters and musical composers who feel compelled to say what they have to say — on canvas or with musical notes — and to say it without any thought of their potential audience. Whether their message is intelligible to their hearers or viewers is of no importance to them. Some, in fact, treat their "public" with contempt.

Preachers cannot afford to be that kind of artist. Being deliberately obtuse or carelessly obscure may be a sign of indifference or even of arrogance. Beginning at a point that is miles from where the congregation is located mentally or spiritually shows little of the sensitivity that preaching requires. Preachers who do not bear their congregation in mind when they prepare their sermons often end up scratching where no one is itching. Or, to change the metaphor, it doesn't matter how loudly we are broadcasting, if no one is tuned in to our frequency.

Preachers should be deeply concerned about how to make their message intelligible to the people who hear it. This means that a sermon cannot be the kind of art that just sits there. In fact, part of the preacher's art has to do with the art of "putting it across." We have known preachers whose voices are monotonous or distracting and have had to attend to the need for modulation and colour in their delivery. We have known others who are physically wooden or who use gestures awkwardly or inappropriately and have benefited from practising in front of a mirror or with videotape. Although this may sound like an issue of skill or technique, it also involves developing our use of the artist's tools.

It is important that the preacher's tools — words, voice, gesture, and so on — be servants and not masters. Again, the aim should not be a well-scripted performance. It is possible to hone our skills to the point that our individual identities — our uniqueness as artists — becomes submerged under a kind of smooth, generic, one-size-fits-all representation of somebody's idea of what all preachers should look and sound like. "Be yourself" and "be the best you can be" are two maxims that need to be kept in careful balance. If you want to preach, develop yourself as fully as you can, but make sure the preacher is still you. Don't lose the authority and authenticity that are uniquely yours. Otherwise, your preaching will not be art.

The passion and the power that mark preaching at its best and are essential to the preacher's art cannot be faked or artificially manufactured. As happens so often, we cannot substitute artifice for art and fool all of the people all of the time. It is when God's message interacts with the preacher's experience in a way that grabs us and shakes us to our foundations that we discover the art of preaching.

1   Jay Weener, "A Word from Jay Weener," *Reformed Review*, 44 (Autumn, 1990): 3–4.

2   Clark, Kenneth, *The Other Half* (Don Mills, Ontario: Longman, 1977), p. 95

Chapter 3

The Art of Music

... art is an event in which the life embodied in an art work and the life of the beholder or performer meet. Music is not a piece of paper with dark spots on it but an experience or, more correctly, an "experiencing." Music as event is about experiencing something — faith, for instance.

— Linda J. Clark, *Music in Churches*[1]

Not all of you who read this chapter will consider yourselves musicians — either professional or amateur. Making music may not be part of your ministry. Yet chances are that as you go about the kinds of ministry to which you are called, you will find yourself rubbing shoulders from time to time with those who practice the art of music. This chapter is for you as well as for them. And it is written by someone who, while he can make his way through a hymn on the piano and has sung in and led choirs over the years, would not consider himself an expert in the field. It is written, though, in the conviction that however musical or unmusical we consider ourselves, there are things we can do to bring a touch of art to our involvement in the music ministry of the church.

The Power of Music

About ten years ago, a young woman in the congregation I was serving went away to a college in North Vancouver to study a subject that, until then, I was only dimly aware of: music therapy. She was an accomplished pianist, and her goal was to prepare herself for a career in which she would use her gift to promote the health and well-being of people. One of the ideas behind music therapy is that, by making music or listening to music, people may be helped to express thoughts and feelings and bring their emotions to the surface. Particularly in situations in which people are ill or distressed or unable to express themselves verbally, music can be used in a therapeutic way.

When we stop to think about it, I don't suppose this should surprise us. In a way, music is therapeutic for many of us. If you play a musical instrument, you may be able to recall times when you sat down at the piano or some other instrument, and just played, and felt the tension of the moment gradually lift from you as you lost yourself in the music. Or perhaps you have a favourite recording. Simply playing it at a time of difficulty can express your feelings and bring release and relief and a sense of peace.

Music therapy is something many of us know a little about, simply through our own experience, but it is also something that people have sensed from time immemorial. Three hundred years ago, William Congreve noted that,

> Music hath charms to soothe the savage breast,
> To soften rocks, or bend a knotted oak.

Centuries earlier, the ancient Greeks expressed the power of music when they said of Orpheus, their god of music, that when he played his lute he had the power to make the trees bow their heads and to change the course of rivers and to tame wild animals.

The earliest biblical example of music's power in a therapeutic setting is found in Samuel I. King Saul, it seems, was subject to fits of depression bordering on madness. As he suffered from this affliction, the order went forth to seek out a man who was skillful in playing the lyre. When the evil spirit fell upon Saul, it was thought, this musician would play on his lyre or harp, and the king would be well. It happened that a member of the court had heard of a young man named David, the son of Jesse, an accomplished musician. Accordingly, David was sought out and brought to the king. "And whenever the evil spirit ... came upon Saul," we're told, "David took the lyre and played it with his hand, and Saul would be relieved and feel better, and the evil spirit would depart from him." (I Samuel 16:23)

The power of music can hardly be denied, but if it can be a power for good, it can also be a power for evil. It can make people whole but, as totalitarian rulers have known, it can also seduce and manipulate people and lead them to their destruction. The folklore of many cultures is rich in stories that illustrate this truth. Germany alone provides two internationally-known stories: that of the Lorelei who lured sailors to their deaths, and the tale of the Pied Piper who, unrewarded after having used his power to charm away the rats, turned his gift against the people of Hamelin and charmed away the children. Martin Luther — who could declare, "Next to theology, I give to music the highest place of honour," and who, for all his thunder and bluster and five-o'clock shadow, sang with a sweet tenor voice — could still feel anxious about the dangers inherent in music's power.

Christians who practice the art of music do well to share Luther's healthy respect for the power of music. Composers, from the greatest to the most humble, have used music as a medium for conveying ideas and emotions. In churches, while few of us write music, many of us have occasion to choose music or to prepare it for use in worship and other settings. What then is the nature of the power of the medium so many of us are exposed to Sunday by Sunday?

Perhaps there is something sacramental about it. In trying to explain the sacraments to people, I sometimes say that, in a sacrament, God communicates with us in a way beyond words. This can be true of music as well. Longfellow called music "the universal language." We don't have to be musically talented or knowledgeable in order for this language to speak to us and touch us deeply.

In his book, *Civilisation*, Kenneth Clark marvels at the phenomenon of Grand Opera. "Why," he asks, "are people prepared to sit silently for three hours listening to a performance of which they do not understand a word and of which they very seldom know the plot? ... Partly, of course, because it is a display of skill, like a football match. But chiefly, I think, because it *is* irrational. 'What is too silly to be said may be sung' — well, yes; but what is too subtle to be said, or too deeply felt, or too revealing, or too mysterious — these things can also be sung and only be sung."[2]

Isn't that the power of music? It is a power to touch and move, to persuade and inspire, to make us laugh and make us weep. Through rhythm and melody the whole range of human feeling can be given a voice. And so we have love songs and work songs, war songs and blue songs, songs to rock a baby to sleep and songs to summon soldiers to action, songs to dance to and songs to march to, songs to bring out the best in us and songs to bring out the worst. If it is true that music can express our deepest feelings and highest aspirations, it is small wonder that music has been used throughout the ages as a vehicle for expressing Christian faith. As Linda Clark says, "Music as event is about experiencing something — faith, for instance."[3] Not just faith either, but the whole range of religious feeling: joy, praise, repentance, commitment, devotion, thanksgiving, sorrow, yearning — it's all there in the literature of Christian music.

Think of the range of expression in just one genre of Christian music: the African American spiritual. From the Blacks of the United States we have everything from the note of triumph in "Ride on, King Jesus," to the note of despair in "Sometimes I Feel Like a Motherless Child"; from the simple praise of "He's Got the Whole World in His Hands," to the dignity and impressive restraint of "Were You There When They Crucified My Lord?" Certainly African Americans have known the range and power of music.

Style and Taste

Anyone who has even a nodding acquaintance with the music program of a church will know instinctively something about the power of music. Just think of the strength of people's reactions to the style of music that is used on Sunday mornings:

> "Why can't we sing more of the old hymns?"
> "Why can't the choir sing something lively and modern instead of those awful old dirges?"

> "The organist plays the prelude so loud I can hardly have a chat with my neighbour."
> "I wish people would stop chattering when the organ is preparing us for worship."

> "Don't you love it when the handbells play in church?"
> "Oh, no, not handbells again!"

The subject of church music rarely comes up without the power of the subject being attested by diverse opinions on matters of taste and aesthetic judgment. It may safely be argued that some kinds of music are "better" than others. If we are concerned that what we sing or play in church should be a fitting offering to God, then the objective quality of the music is something that deserves our attention.

Even so, it should be only one consideration. There are purists — including not a few organists — who bridle at being asked to play something they quite rightly regard as inferior music. Some simply refuse to go along with it. Others attempt to raise the quality of the piece by means of the way they play it.

I remember an intergenerational service that began with the hymn, "Part of the Family." Now, no one would claim that the piece is great music. The organist for the service found its calliope-style "oom-pah-pah" rhythm downright hokey. So he tried to smooth it all out by improvising an accompaniment that made it sound like a rather staid, nineteenth-century hymn. It didn't work!

Our pursuit of excellence in worship makes it a legitimate goal of a music director to educate the congregation and develop its taste. But there is also a place in worship for music that is less than excellent — as well as performances that are less than excellent — especially when other factors like the message of the words and the music's function in drawing people together have a significant part to play. Similarly, there is a place for hymns with less than excellent words; there may, within reason and good judgement, be occasions when other considerations make it permissible to use a hymn with language that is less inclusive than we might wish. In the case of music that is of lesser quality, it is important that it be rendered — as that rendition of "Part of the Family" was not — in an appropriate style, the style in which the piece was intended to be played or sung. It's important, in other words, to meet the music on its own terms.

Of course, we sometimes make the mistake of assuming that the best music is the most difficult or complicated or sophisticated music. Some churches can get a bit snooty about their music programs. Yet I remember a tenor soloist singing the spiritual "His Eye Is On The Sparrow" one Sunday in a church that was used to a diet of Bach and Mozart. It is a simple song, and the soloist sang it with the disarming simplicity it required. It was the most memorable thing in the service.

The word for what we're talking about is integrity. Music of whatever quality needs to be performed in a way that is true to itself. And the acid test in choosing music appropriate for Christian worship may be the truth that it conveys. As Linda Clark says, "aesthetic judgments entail judgments about candour — how true to life the art work is — and about craft — how well the art work is done or performed."[4]

Coherence and Congruence

The word "integrity" suggests a "holding together." It implies the need for things to be integrated, to hold together to produce a satisfying whole. Other words with overtones of that same idea are "coherence" and "congruence." People who select music for worship services need to be familiar with these concepts, too.

"Coherence" is a concept that I use in two senses. First, a worship service needs to have coherence in the sense that the various elements in the service cohere or hang together. Those who choose music for a service and who believe that there is an art to that task will, for the most part, try to choose music that relates to the theme or themes of the service. A hymn or an anthem will not appear as an interruption in the flow of the service, but will contribute to a larger conception.

It is sometimes said of the American musical theatre that the first musical in which song and dance advanced the plot was Rodgers and Hammerstein's "Oklahoma!" Until then, most musicals were like reviews into which songs were "dropped." Songs were merely vehicles for this or that singer to show her stuff; they didn't necessarily have a lot to do with the plot. All that changed with "Oklahoma!"

In the same way, the music in a worship service should "advance the plot" — or at least help underscore a theme or move the service along.

The other sense in which coherence is important is in the way in which music — like the other elements in worship — should relate to the actual experience of the worshippers. As we have said before, it is important that worship relate to the realities of people's lives. For the music in a service to do that, it needs to be accessible. It needs to be within people's reach. That is not to say that it shouldn't challenge people or stretch them in some way, but it should be attainable. To be art, the music we use in worship needs to have a message, but it also needs to be a message that people will recognize — or at least one that they can hear.

Then what about that other word? "Congruence" is a word I'm using in a narrower sense. Much of the music we use in worship has words to it: hymns, anthems, sung responses, and so on. Just as it is important for the music in worship to have cohesion — to hang together with the rest of the service and with people's lived experience — it is important for the words of a piece of music to be congruent with the music itself. In other words, it is important not only for the words to fit the music, but for the music to suit the words.

Where this becomes a practical issue is in the choosing of an alternate tune to use for the words of a hymn. Many of us have had the experience of wanting to use the words of a hymn in the Hymn Book but of finding that they are set to an unfamiliar tune. Those of us who are acquainted with the metrical index at the back of the book know that we can find other tunes to which we can sing these words simply by checking the metre of the tune where the words appear (usually listed at the top or bottom of the page) against the same metre in the metrical index. The index will provide a list of other tunes to the same metre, at least one of which may be more familiar to the congregation.

Knowing how to use the metrical index is a skill, but there is an art to finding a tune that both fits the right number of notes to the right number of syllables and actually suits the words. Not every tune will do that. Some tunes may seem stark and abrupt, when the words are begging for something that is gently flowing. If the words you are using speak of sorrow and loss, a sprightly tune may not be appropriate. If the words are about the joy of resurrection, a mournful tune in a minor key will sound incongruous. There may, in other words, be a lack of congruence between the words and the music. If we want to find something where the music will enhance the message of the words and vice versa, we will need to be sensitive to the need for congruence.

The Congregation's Musical Culture

There is something else to which we will need to be sensitive — or rather, two things that we will need to keep in balance. Those of us who have responsibility for choosing music for worship services will want our choices to reflect our own integrity, our sense of what is theologically valid, verbally appropriate and musically fitting — but we will also want to take into account what might be called the musical culture of the congregation.

Musical culture is something that can manifest itself in a number of ways. Church musicians and "ordered" ministers have had the experience of moving from one congregation to another and discovering that the second church sings the words of a familiar hymn to a different tune from the one the minister is used to. That's an example of a congregation's musical culture, and it's important for the musician or minister to recognize its reality! Musical culture may also be reflected in the kind of choral singing that takes place in the Sunday service. In one church it may be old Gospel favorites; in another it may be anthems and service music in the Anglican cathedral style.

Musical culture — especially when there are words to be sung — can be more complex than these examples may indicate. As we suggested earlier, it is not uncommon for a congregation to include people who have differing views about musical styles, about whether, for example, to sing only old, familiar hymns or to introduce something new each week. Those who are put in a position of having to choose music are often subject to countervailing pressures that may take the form of criticism from one person over the choice of a hymn that was conspicuously lacking in inclusive language and from another person over why we have to sing this inclusive language stuff at all.

I was once cornered by a church member who had taken umbrage at an inclusive-language doxology that we had sung the previous Sunday. Having got some of her distress out of her system, she relented slightly and added, "But then I guess you're getting a lot of pressure from these people; it must be hard to keep them happy." It was at that point that I had to say, "Well, I do have a few convictions of my own, you know."

And that, I think, is an example of personal integrity and the congregation's musical culture meeting head-to-head. On the one hand are the congregation's culture and comfort-level — a culture that may be complex and a comfort-level that will not be the same for everyone. The worship leader needs to be sensitive to these realities and not simply impose his/her own tastes and values on them. The music, after all, is to be *everyone's* opportunity to express something of their faith. If the person who chooses the anthems and hymns disregards the people's legitimate need to do this, or if s/he uses his/her power exclusively to make people sing the words s/he thinks will improve their theology or the tunes s/he thinks will improve their musical taste, s/he may begin to notice a marked lack of participation on the part of the congregation.

On the other hand there is the music-chooser's need to consult his/her own convictions. That person may rightly feel, for example, that to "cave in" to a steady diet of hymns whose words and music express themes like militarism and religious triumphalism (the idea of Christianity as an irresistible expansionist movement) would be to allow ourselves to become more and more distant from the realities of our time and the values of Christian faith today. Again, what is needed is balance. And those who want to apply artistic values to the task of choosing music for worship will want to pay attention both to the message that they want to bring to the congregation's consciousness and to the life experiences the congregation brings to the service of worship. Both deserve to be considered.

The complexity of the congregation's consciousness and culture requires open-mindedness on the part of worshippers to those who may have a different point of view. To those who complain that we don't sing enough of the old hymns, I would say: Don't forget that every hymn you know was new to you at one time. Try to be open to both the words and the music of pieces that may be new to you. There may be some new insight in them for you. Or you may find yourself being touched in a way that hasn't happened for you before.

To those who complain that older hymns use inappropriate language and outmoded theology, I would say: Don't forget that music operates at a subtle level. You might not want to encourage a mindless kind of nostalgia that distances people from the realities of modern life. On the other hand, resist the temptation to roll your eyes when the family asks that "In The Garden" be sung at Grandma's funeral. No, it isn't good theology, and it isn't great music; but it may be a good example of the way music evokes memories and associations for people that go beyond the notes and the words on the page. And it may be reason enough to set aside our critical faculties on occasion and let the people sing for reasons that go beyond the intrinsic value of the words and the music themselves.

To those who complain that we don't sing enough of that up-beat music that we heard at the church conference, I would say: Introduce some of it, by all means. But don't be too quick to replace all of the old stuff. Remember that the music of faith is something that, for many people, and more than any other medium, connects them to other periods of their lives and provides a theme of continuity for their faith journey. Not long ago I worshipped in an unfamiliar church on Mother's Day. In front of me sat an elderly mother with her adult son. Half way through "I Love to Tell the Story," she began to weep. What chord had been struck, what set of sympathetic vibrations that hymn had set in motion for her, I have no idea, but obviously it went deep — as music so often can do. Whatever the critics may think of the hymn, I'm glad she was given an opportunity to sing it.

Specifics

As with the chapter on worship, we conclude these thoughts about the art of music with some comments about specific elements in our worship services in which music plays a part.

Instrumental Music

It is said of Erik Routley, the English Congregational minister, organist and hymnologist, that the minister of a church where he was organist once asked him to improvise something to cover up the pitter-patter of little feet as the children left for their Sunday school classes. "No," Routley replied slowly and thoughtfully, "No, I don't think I'll do that. Why don't you just mumble something?"

Routley's point is well-taken. In this era of "muzak" in which we are used to hearing — or, rather, not hearing — a background wash of music played in elevators and supermarkets, we may think that it is appropriate for instrumental music in churches to take on a similarly bland and inconspicuous role. Congregations with organists who use the instrument for what sounds suspiciously like self-glorification might wish that the music were more bland and inconspicuous than it is! We need to consider how to avoid either extreme.

In the context of worship, the organ — if that is the primary instrument in use — is there to lead and support the musical praise of God. That is something that should be done in a clear, unapologetic but not overbearing way. The need for clarity leads an organist friend of mine to suggest that if a congregation cannot afford even a cabinet pipe organ, it should consider a good piano as an alternative to a second-rate electric or electronic organ.

Then what of the times when the organ is not leading or accompanying choral or congregational singing? Most services begin with a prelude that should be chosen with its purpose in mind: the preparation of the people for worship. And the congregation needs to keep this purpose in mind as well, and provide enough quiet for the prelude to be heard and do its work rather than providing background music for the weekly gossip-and-catching-up chatter.

The second point at which we are most likely to hear the organ alone is during the Offertory. Again, our understanding of the Offertory's purpose should not be that the organ is played in order to cover up or distract us from this unseemly intrusion into the service, but to help us to meditate on what we are offering in a way that reminds us that this, too, is an act of worship.

The Postlude is often seen as the moment for the virtuoso organist to shine. While it may often be appropriate for the congregation to be sent out with a flourish, other considerations still need to be subordinated to the theme of the service and the purpose of worship in general when the Postlude is chosen.

Instruments other than organs and pianos are sometimes used in worship. When a guitar is used for rhythmic accompaniment, care should be taken that the melodic lead is given clearly, so that the congregation can join in with confidence. When other instruments, like handbells, play a selection on their own, the questions that need to be asked include: How does this particular selection contribute to the overall effect and purpose of the service? Is there coherence between this selection and the theme, or does it seem to be simply a diversion or a novelty?

Choirs

The fact that choir practices generally devote much more time to rehearsing anthems than to going over the hymns for Sunday sometimes obscures the fact that the choir's primary purpose is to lead the congregational singing. When a choir makes a great impression in Sunday worship by singing a challenging anthem but does not seem sufficiently familiar with one of the hymns or an item of service music to give the congregation a good, strong lead, that choir has its priorities backwards. Most choirs find that their leadership role is fulfilled most effectively if they sing the first verse of a hymn in unison, breaking into parts only at the second verse. If the organist is able to vary the harmonies on the last verse, the choir, of course, reverts to unison.

It should be remembered that the choir's leadership role is not limited to singing. Think of the difference it makes when the choir gives the congregation a clear cue by standing at the beginning of the last line of music when a hymn is being played over rather than straggling uncertainly to its feet. When you consider that most choirs may be heard for only a few minutes in the service but are seen from beginning to end, perhaps you will understand how important their deportment is, how influential their body language. They can convey the message that the service is an important occasion or that they would just as soon be catching an extra forty winks, that the sermon is worthy of attention or that it could be easily dispensed with, that this is a community that pulls together or a collection of individuals each with his or her own agenda.

Choirs other than the main service choir — junior choirs, youth choirs, folk music choirs, and so on — often give the impression of being brought on to do their "turn" and then leaving the "stage." Would they not appear to be more integrated into the service if they were given more to do? They could lead one of the hymns for example, or take part in a litany or responsive reading. Anything that mitigates the "slotted-in" look would contribute to a sense of "art" about their contribution to the service.

The anthems themselves — regardless of which choir is singing them — should be sung to texts appropriate for the occasion. And thought should be given to where best to place them in each service. Rather than thinking in terms of an "anthem slot," why not let the text suggest where best to place the choral piece? If it is a psalm text, why not put it in place of the responsive reading? If it is a prayer, why not use it as an introit into the prayers of the day? If it is set to scripture, why not place it among the lessons? If it sounds like an invitation to worship, why not move it to the beginning of the service? Again the question to ask is, How can this particular item best contribute to the experience of worship as a whole?

Congregational Singing

There was a time when the singing of hymns was not only the most important way in which Protestant congregations actively participated in worship; it was virtually the *only* way in which they participated. Almost everything else was a monologue by the pastor. Times have changed, but the singing of hymns and responses remains a significant part of the "liturgy" — literally, "the people's work."

If the organist (or pianist) and choir do their "work" by giving strong leadership, the people will be able to do their work well, too. It is important for the congregation to be able to feel confident about their singing. This means that, if a hymn or sung response is unfamiliar, the congregation is encouraged to make friends with it by having it carefully introduced and rehearsed. We all know what a "downer" it can be to be asked to sing "cold" something we don't know by someone who either thought we knew it or simply didn't think through the consequences of their choice. The congregation can feel incompetent and alienated and distracted from the business of worship. The worship leader may have to work hard to regain their sympathy and attention. For the same reason, it is good to use the same setting of a sung response (a "Sanctus," for example, or an "Alleluia" after the Assurance of Pardon) for several weeks in a row or for a liturgical season, so that people really feel comfortable with it. This is far preferable to switching to something new every week.

We may not want to encourage people to be such creatures of habit that they go through worship with their minds "in neutral," but neither do we want to leave them feeling that there is nothing in the service that comes naturally to them, or that the service belongs to the leaders but not to the people. Once again we come back to the need for those who choose the music to develop the art of keeping in balance the need for selecting hymns that carry the appropriate message with the need to respect the interests of those who will be called upon to sing them.

1   Linda J. Clark, *Music in Churches* (Washington: Alban Institute, 1994), p. xi.

2   Kenneth Clark, *Civilisation* (London: BBC and John Murray, 1969), p. 243.

3   Clark, Linda J., p. xi.

4   Clark, Linda J., p. 69.

Chapter 4

The Art of Administering The Rites

It is said of the great ballerina, Pavlova, that after her performance in a ballet someone asked her what a particular dance had meant. "Do you think I would have danced it," she replied, "if I could have said it?"

— F. W. Dillistone, *Jesus Christ and His Cross*[1]

We've all heard the expression that actions speaker louder than words. Sometimes words and actions together have a power that either of them alone can lack. In administering the two sacraments recognized by most Protestants (Baptism and Holy Communion) and in conducting rites of passage associated with the church (Baptism again, Confirmation, Marriage and Funeral or Memorial Services), those who plan and lead such services have an opportunity to use both words and actions in a way that is art.

Though most denominations specify that professional staff carry out a certain role in these rites, the part played by congregational lay leadership is becoming increasingly important. There is art in the interaction of people, in the way the leadership team at a baptism or confirmation relate to each other and to those participating in the rite.

Each of the public acts we are considering in this chapter carries a message — a message rooted in human experience and in Christian theology. Each uses a variety of media and symbolic elements and gestures. For example, we may sprinkle water in Baptism, break bread and pour wine in Communion, lay on hands at Confirmation, bless and exchange rings in Marriage, and place earth on a coffin prior to burial. We may be less trusting than Pavlova that the "manual acts" speak for themselves, and so our actions are usually accompanied by words to clarify their meaning. And our words are spoken and our acts are performed in relation to a specific audience — a congregation that we hope will be able to understand these expressions of art.

As with other acts of worship, these services require that thought be given to the three elements we have just mentioned: the content of the message we wish to convey, the nature of the media we are called on to use, and the question of where the people in the congregation "are at" so that we can convey the message and use the media in ways that will touch their experience.

The messages that our sacraments and other rites carry will necessarily be informed by the theology of our denomination — and by our own personal theological emphases. In Baptism, the language we choose will indicate whether we have chosen to emphasize water's cleansing or life-giving properties. Our theology of atonement will be expressed in the words of the Great Thanksgiving prayer that we write or choose for Communion. The wording of the vows we use at a wedding will reflect our theology of marriage. And so on. If art is to convey a message, we need to consider carefully what the message is to be.

Art has to do as well with how we convey the message. The presider's manner and demeanour speak just as loudly as the words used. Those of us who have a part to play in these dramas need to ask ourselves whether we communicate a degree of grace in the way we conduct our share of the service. Do we prepare sufficiently so that the rite progresses smoothly? Do we anticipate what props we will need so that they will be where we want them when they are needed? Are we familiar enough with the procedures that we can cope with unexpected developments without appearing to be totally taken off guard? If particular gestures are appropriate (for example, the use of hands in invoking the Holy Spirit during the eucharistic prayer at Communion), do we take care that our gestures are not awkward or abrupt, but fluid and gracious?

You might think that getting people's names right would be pretty basic to our carrying off a service with a degree of grace and art. And yet, how often is this basic element neglected — and what message do we give people when it is? Years ago I remember attending a marriage service at which the officiant referred to the bride and groom repeatedly as "Murray and Lorna." Their names were Larry and Myrna. What does it do to the sense of occasion at a funeral when the presider fails to call the deceased by the correct name?

And yet these things are known to happen. And when they do, even the least alert worshipper will rightly sense a lack of art in the way in which the service is conducted.

Mention of the worshippers reminds me that the third element the artist needs to be aware of — in this case the audience or congregation that attends an occasional service — often includes many people who are not regular worshippers. This is obviously true when we think of services that do not take place on a Sunday morning — weddings and funerals, for example. But even Baptisms and Confirmations, which take place in the context of regular worship, can attract friends and family members of the candidates — people who may not have frequent exposure to Christian culture. In what ways do we consider the thoughts and feelings and experiences of these people as we plan the service and frame the message? As artists we need to think about both the integrity of what we have to say and the reality of the audience that we are addressing.

Bringing a touch of art to the sacraments and ordinances of the church begins with some basic "do's" and "don'ts." Asked for some basic advice about baptizing infants, an experienced minister once told a young ordinand simply, "Don't drop the baby." To convey a message of God's grace through the way we conduct one of these rites, we will need to go a bit further than that! Perhaps it's time for us to consider these occasional services — if only briefly — one by one.

Baptism

The majority of baptismal candidates in our mainline churches are infants, and the comments you will find in this section are made with that reality in mind.

Over the past few decades, many local congregations have introduced policies on Baptism. This is a positive development, especially if the committees responsible for framing these policies have asked themselves what message they believe the sacrament should convey. Our words around the water, for example, will be chosen according to one set of criteria if we see the baptismal water as a cleansing agent; they will be chosen differently if we see the water in terms of its life-giving properties; or we may understand baptism simply as a rite of invitation and membership. What we do and say may vary according to whether we wish to put our emphasis on God's grace or on a human response of faith and commitment. What we do with the

Trinitarian formula ("I baptize you in the name of the Father, and of the Son, and of the Holy Spirit") will indicate whether we value more highly our ecumenical connections to the larger church or our conviction that feminine/female imagery needs to be included in our expression of the Divine.

An infinite number of policy decisions convey a message of one kind or another. For instance, whether we allow private Baptisms in the chapel on a Sunday afternoon or insist that the sacrament take place in the context of regular Sunday worship will say something about how we see the congregation's role in this covenant. Is it a congregational event or a private rite of passage? How we handle requests for Baptism from non-resident families (typically, where the young parents have moved away but the grandparents still live in the community) makes a statement, as well. The role we ascribe to godparents (whether they are required or permitted or excluded, whether they make promises or remain silent) also speaks of the meaning and significance of this act. Whether or not we require sponsors to take part when neither parent is a confirmed member of the church will speak about where we come down between the poles of openness ("Whosoever will may come") and an expectation of seriousness on the part of those who present their children for Baptism. What preparation and follow-up we provide for parents will reflect our beliefs about the church's responsibility for education and pastoral care.

In many ways, decisions will have been made about the message we intend to convey even before a particular baptismal service is planned. Within the service itself, however, all kinds of opportunities are available to communicate messages through the media of words and actions. In each case the particular audience — a mixture of regular worshippers and visitors — needs to be considered.

If Baptism is seen as a declaration of God's grace and as a formal rite of passage into the Christian community, it may be good to take advantage of this opportunity to dramatize the diversity of that community. The children of the church can be involved in a way that allows them to welcome a new brother or sister in Christ. This could include having a child carrying the water vessel lead the procession of families, or having the children of the Sunday school sing an appropriate song, or involving children in the presentation of a gift at the conclusion of the ceremony. The welcoming of the child to the congregation in general can include not only asking covenantal questions of the people but carrying the child into the midst of the assembly as a sign of inclusion.

The choice of symbols beyond the water itself needs to strike a balance between the traditional symbols of Christian faith and those that will be accessible to people who live in a predominantly secular culture. The oil of chrism, for instance, may have an honourable pedigree in the Christian tradition (although one may question its introduction in denominations that have neglected it for a long period), but it is a difficult symbol to use in our current context without a good deal of explanation. At the other extreme, gifts of books or plants may be things that people today can understand, but their place in Christian tradition is less clear; hence they may not convey as cogent a Christian message. The choice of a candle may be a good one; "light" is not only a symbol that abounds in scriptural tradition, but it is one that does well at speaking for itself to a modern audience.

Through the entire baptismal service, nothing will convey a message as clearly as the presider's voice and demeanour. Depending on "how it is done," the presider — intentionally or otherwise — can convey a number of messages: that this event is important or trivial, that it is shallow and sentimental ("Aren't these babies cute?") or profound and far-reaching ("God has created them and wishes to be known by them"), that the families are welcome or a darned nuisance, that the congregation is an essential part of what is happening or a group of passive onlookers. Graciousness on the part of the presider — especially in the face of howling babies — can convey a message of grace from God.

Confirmation

In Confirmation, the historic faith of the church becomes personal. Young people and an increasing proportion of adults come forward to profess their faith. Here is an opportunity for the candidates and the presider to work together at developing a rite that will allow the candidates both to associate themselves publicly with the faith and mission of the church and to express something of their own experience of these things. When these two elements come together in a way that informs and inspires the congregation at large, something takes place that has a touch of art about it.

In answering the church's questions about faith and commitment, in joining in the reading of a creed, in having laid on them the hands of those in whom the church has invested a representative function (a presiding minister and a member of the church board, for instance), candidates for confirmation link themselves to the Christian community past and present. But these standard acts may be augmented in ways that help to tell the personal stories of each candidate. For example, those who are baptized as adults or confirmed may be given an opportunity to make their own statement of faith or to describe something of their "faith journey." Those who lay on hands may include not only those who take part in a representative capacity, but individuals who have been chosen because they have helped to shape the candidate's faith. As well as the standard laying on of hands (symbolic of the gift of the Holy Spirit) and the repeated use of the same formula of words for each candidate, additional symbols can be presented to the candidates — identical symbols that may suggest the ministry we all share, or different ones specific to the gifts that each person brings.

In Confirmation, as in Baptism, the words and symbols we use should reflect the message we wish to convey and should be accessible to those who witness the event and participate in it.

Holy Communion

While Baptism and Confirmation are Christian rites of passage, observed only once for each candidate, Holy Communion (or the Lord's Supper or Eucharist) is the community meal to which all the baptized are admitted again and again. (It used to be that Communion was given to a person for the first time following Confirmation, but increasingly it is offered to any baptized person who is old enough to have some understanding of its significance.)

This is not the place for an exhaustive discussion of sacramental theology — let alone the great variety of sacramental theologies that prevail among our churches. Certainly the message we intend to convey in the sacrament of Communion must begin with our theological understanding of this act's significance. Beyond that "given" we can at least say some things about the message we convey in the *way* we do it.

Think, for example, of what we say when we choose intinction over receiving the bread and wine in the pews. Does coming forward to receive the elements suggest a different emphasis from being served by our neighbour in the pew? Does eating and drinking individually convey something different from the practice of waiting until all have been served and communicating simultaneously? Are pre-cut cubes of bread a more or less effective symbol of what we want to say than bread torn from a single loaf? And again, what about the demeanour of those — lay and clergy — who may be involved in conducting the service and serving the elements? Do they give the impression that this is a significant act without looking funereal; do they manage to look celebrative without appearing slip-shod and excessively casual. Striking the right balance is not easy. Yet it is possible for us to lend dignity to the occasion without appearing stiff or nervous. (At a church I used to know, the Communion servers did everything with such military precision that they all but clicked their heels when they turned a right angle. There would have been more grace and art in the service if they could have relaxed a bit.)

It is as we think of some of the choices celebrants and worship committees need to make about how Communion is served, that we begin to see clearly what an important part the "audience," the congregation, plays in these decisions. A minister may have some wonderful ideas about increasing the frequency of celebrating Communion, the worship committee may want to change the way in which the elements are received, but many of their plans founder on the rocks of congregational resistance and practical problems. Congregations often have a big investment in the meaning they perhaps unconsciously associate with the way things have always been done. If they suspect, again unconsciously, that a change in method implies a change in meaning, they may well not be receptive to the unfamiliar ways of doing things. If those who offer leadership are clear about the message they wish to communicate and are convinced of its validity, they may well apply these modifications to the art-form known as Communion, but they should proceed with caution and an abundance of patience and sensitivity.

The "manual acts" in Communion, and any changes to them, will often catch the attention of a congregation. No less significant, but sometimes harder for the average worshipper to spot, are changes to the words. In an age when many thoughtful people are reassessing their theology of the sacrament — the nature of atonement, the import of the "body-and-blood" imagery, the place of suffering and sacrifice in human life — efforts are being made in some quarters to modify traditional language and to re-cast the words of the Great Thanksgiving or eucharistic prayer.

It is here that some advice from the American liturgical scholar, James White, seems relevant. In the midst of the liturgical experiments of the

1970s, White entitled a chapter of one of his books, "You Are Free — If."[2] His point was that we should feel free to make changes if we "know what is essential in any type of worship,"[3] if we understand the basics, if we know the background, if we know what we are doing. Unfortunately some people have taken a very cavalier approach to the eucharistic prayer and made up something that may express the individual celebrant's beliefs but ignores the received traditions of the church. It is consistent with White's caution, I think, to suggest that the basic elements of the Great Thanksgiving should all be present: the Peace, Sursum Corda, Thanksgiving for Creation and Providence, references to Jesus' life and ministry, a recollection of the upper room, invocation of the Holy Spirit, words of self-dedication. If we understand the basic structure and flow of the prayer, it may be quite legitimate for us to take up the challenge of expressing these various elements in ways that are informed by a living theology. It is important to bear in mind, however, that this prayer is not a prayer of an individual but a prayer of the church; the community — locally, denominationally and ecumenically — should be involved in producing and approving materials that express the community's voice.

Marriage

I know ministers who would say that weddings are the bane of their existence. Meeting with couples who have little or no connection to the church, directing unruly mobs at wedding rehearsals, performing the weddings before congregations of strangers, attending tedious wedding receptions and being regaled with all-too-familiar stories of the groom's drinking prowess — the whole experience can leave a minister feeling like a glorified civil servant, or like a minor player in some family's social extravaganza or, worst of all, like someone who is obliged to function in a way that feels like misusing his/her time and prostituting his/her abilities and services.

It should not be surprising that some clergy resent the time they give to weddings and all that goes with them. As long as the performing of marriages remains one of the things the church does, however, we can choose between going through the motions and conducting these services with integrity.

The issue of integrity, of course, is one that needs to be raised long before the bride comes down the aisle. Before the church commits itself to a particular wedding, it is good for the officiant to meet with the couple to hear about what is important to them in terms of where and how they are married. It is good, too, if the minister can explain what is important to the church — what expectations the church may have, such as attending services or enrolling in a marriage preparation course. It is important for the couple to understand how essential it is that they be married in a way that has integrity for them — a way that reflects their beliefs and values. The minister has a responsibility to explain what integrity means for her/him, too, so that plans for this wedding can go ahead at this church only if the things that have integrity for the couple and the things that have integrity for the minister are compatible. When that is the case, three people can plan the service in such a way that it can carry a message that reflects an agreed upon point of view — and in a way that may be called art.

Even when there is a sense of compatibility between presider and couple, the church's representative may find that, in marriage services more than in any of the others we are considering in this chapter, the church's values come up against the values of secular society. In the symbols that are used, in the music that is selected, in the supplementary (non-scriptural) readings that the couple requests, in the struggle between ostentation and simplicity — in all these issues, a sense of integrity can be put to the test.

Nevertheless, those who represent the church in this collaboration do well to remember that the couple has voluntarily chosen to approach this congregation with their request, and it is the church that hosts the marriage. The church, therefore, has the last word on what takes place in its place of worship. At the very least, the marriage service is an opportunity for the church to bring the good news of God's intention for us, to challenge the congregation to think about the quality of their own relationships, and to expand our understanding of marriage from a private arrangement between the two principals to an institution with social dimensions and social responsibilities. Of course, there is no point in presenting a Christian perspective on these issues in a way that alienates an unfamiliar audience because it seems irrelevant or judgmental or just plain unattractive. This is an opportunity to represent the Christian community to what may be a largely unchurched constituency. Both the importance of the message and the nature of the audience need to be gauged carefully if appropriate words and other media are to be found to carry the truth we have to tell.

One detail of the planning of the service that deserves comment in this section concerns the wording of the vows. The 1960s, when couples often insisted on writing their own marriage vows, are long gone. Some, however, still ask about finding alternatives to the vows suggested to them or ask if they can have a crack at writing their own. In these situations, my response usually reflects the advice of James White: "You are free [to change things] — *if*."[4] As long as the essential elements are there (a reference to God and other witnesses, promises that are not contingent on favourable circumstances, a promise of fidelity, and the expression of a life-long intention), then let's talk. Individualize the vows by all means, but don't lose sight of the essential elements that the Christian community values.

Funerals and Memorial Services

As with weddings, being called on to conduct a funeral or a memorial service can bring a minister into the lives of people who may not be affiliated with the congregation. Whether the deceased or his/her family are active in the church or not, the service will almost surely be attended by people who are not regular worshippers.

A member of a church where I was once minister sympathized with me at having to go into the homes of people I didn't know and being expected to put together a service for a member of their family. She imagined I must resent this apparent imposition. I replied that, while the task could be difficult, it is also a privilege to be invited into people's lives at such a vulnerable time and to be included in their conversation as they recall the life they have known and try to express what it has meant to them.

Funerals and memorial services are another time when the message the church has to offer — the good news of God's gift of life and of a divine love that cannot be defeated by death — comes together with the specific experience of individuals and families. As with some of the other rites we have examined in this chapter, the perceived needs and perspectives of the people we deal with are sometimes in a creative tension with the word we are called to speak.

In putting together a service to mark a death, some churches and some individual clergy emphasize the continuity of the Gospel message to the point of varying the service hardly at all from one funeral to the next. Personal references to the life of the one who has died may be few; in fact, the individual's name may hardly be mentioned. This approach stresses the function of the funeral, not as a private affair, but as a witness to the communion of saints. The emphasis is on grief and resurrection and the message is that, although we live as individuals in this life, we all become one in God after death.

At the other extreme are services in which the sermon is essentially replaced by a eulogy that leaves the impression that the deceased's life was so blameless — or his faith so unassailable — that God would not dare to deny him entry to heaven. Such services, I think, cater to what the presider imagines the congregation wants to hear — and neglects an opportunity to proclaim a message that they need to hear.

A service, which should be planned by the presider and the bereaved together, should strive to blend what is good news for us all with a recognition of the uniqueness of the life that has been lived. Through scripture readings and the hymns of the faith, the continuity of the church's message is expressed. Through a spoken personal appreciation by a friend or family member and through the use of pictures or symbols that recall some aspect of the deceased's life or character, recognition is given to the fact that this life was like no other and has left its own particular mark.

There are places in the service, of course, where the tension between Christian theology on the one hand and the specific beliefs of the deceased or the bereaved present us with a very real challenge. The beliefs of the people to whom we minister at a time of death may be more eclectic than a specifically Christian faith would hold. They may, for example, be influenced by what we could call "civic religion." When it comes to beliefs about life after death, for instance, the mourners' ideas may be more in tune with the Greek idea of the immortality of the soul than they are with the Judeo-Christian idea of the resurrection of the body. The sermon is an opportunity for the preacher to proclaim a message that emphasizes the gift of God's grace rather than the inherent right of our souls to go marching on. When such a message is joined with an affirmation of the genuine humanity of the deceased's earthly life, we may feel that we are conducting a service that has integrity as an act of Christian worship.

Funerals and memorial services are occasions when it is important for Christian officiants to be clear about the message they have to proclaim. The cultural assaults on this specifically Christian proclamation can be many and subtle. They go beyond the family's own predilections to the values upheld by funeral directors, which may not be the same as those upheld by the church, to the theology inherent in the rites of fraternal organizations, which may be at variance with a genuinely Christian perspective on matters of life and death. When a religion follows a founder for whom death was a painful reality, we sell our message short if we go along with efforts to deny or sentimentalize this reality. The Gospel is good news only because it dares to stare death in the face and still speak a word of life and hope.

Of course, grief requires a pastoral response. It is not a time to blow people's beliefs out of the water simply because they are shallow or sentimental. Some funeral manuals seem to be based on a rather heartless brand of Christianity that shows little compassion for real people. No doubt some expressions of rigidity are a response to society's attempts to water down the distinctiveness of the word Christianity can bring to the experience of loss through death. For the rituals we perform following a death to be truly art, we need to be true to the message entrusted to us and to convey it in a way that will persuade those who mourn that God and the church do really care.

1   F. W. Dillistone, *Jesus Christ and His Cross* (London: Lutterworth Press, 1953), p. 139.

2   James F. White, *Christian Worship in Transition* (Nashville: Abingdon, 1976), p. 10.

3   *Ibid.*

4   *Ibid.*

Chapter 5

The Art of Pastoral Care

MOYERS: But how do you bring mystery and art together with science?

DELBANCO: Let me give you a musical analogy. If I'm going to play the violin, I have to know some very concrete things. I have to know where to put my fingers, how to draw the bow, how hard to push, how quickly to draw, and so forth. To a certain degree there's a science of violin playing. But if I want to make the music really speak to you, then I have to do something that goes beyond just these mechanics. Medicine is no different from that. I've got to go beyond the technical aspects of this test and that part of your body. I've got to somehow try to understand your spirit and maybe even touch it at times.

— Thomas Delbanco, M. D., in conversation with Bill Moyers[1]

Science and mystery; technique and art. Bill Moyers' television series and book, *Healing and the Mind*, explored some of the connections between these things. He found a number of seminal thinkers in the field of health care — people who are often seen as scientists and technicians — affirming the fact that the connections with mystery and art are both real and crucial. This should say something to those of us who have an interest in pastoral care.

All of us in the church, clergy and lay, are involved in pastoral care. Visiting someone in hospital, listening to a troubled friend, writing a note to someone who has lost a loved one: these are things that all of us do either occasionally or frequently. Whether we have been equipped by special training as caregivers or not, we are all called upon at times to offer care to someone else. We hope that our contacts with people will be received as expressions of concern and will have an element of healing in them.

Those who have been prepared for ordered ministry and those who have received other kinds of training for caregiving know that there are techniques that can be developed for use in pastoral care. We can learn various listening techniques, for example, in order to draw a person out and encourage her or him to say more. We can train ourselves to see beneath the "presenting problem" to the real issue that concerns a person. We can develop advocacy skills so that we can intercede on behalf of hospital patients who feel that their questions are not being answered. But our repertoire of techniques can seem coldly professional if it is not clothed in art. In fact, a virtuoso performance of our skills can leave a person feeling merely like an object of pastoral care. Real care will be experienced and real healing will be sensed only when we can replace artfulness with art.

Where does the art, the mystery, lie? Thomas Delbanco, a medical doctor, locates it in the doctor-patient relationship. Similarly, Father Thomas Dailey, Director of the St. Joseph's College Bioethics Centre in Edmonton, Alberta, has said that pastoral care becomes art when it has something "extra" in it. That "extra," says Dailey, is a relationship of trust in which the caregiver becomes a significant other and allows the patient to speak.[2]

The Mutuality of Pastoral Care

For several months I visited a woman in hospital who had suffered a severe stroke. Even with therapy, her vocabulary never again extended beyond a dozen words. Yet her mind was alert, and as a result her life was full of frustration. Conversations were necessarily limited. Each time I saw her, I told her how much these visits meant to me. This woman taught me about the preciousness and fragility of life and about how some of the deepest things of life can be communicated in silence. I learned something about the value of touch when it is given with permission. I felt that the patient ministered to me.

Exciting things happen in pastoral care when the visitor goes as one human being to another. When the visitor goes expecting to receive as well as to give and willing to share his or her own feelings honestly, both parties may experience care and healing.

Many of us have gone to see someone who was sick or troubled, wondering what we could possibly say to them. And we have often ended the visit feeling humbled and inspired by the spirit of the person we have visited. We have found that we have received more than we have given. Both the visitor and the visited can find a sense of care when each is expectant and open to the gifts the other has to offer.

Trust Based on Honesty

Several years ago, I visited a woman younger than myself in hospital. She had cancer and was not expected to live long. As a visitor, I felt uncomfortable in her presence and guilty that I had every prospect of going on living while she was condemned to die. I felt I had to be honest with her about how I was feeling. As I expressed my awkwardness, she seemed to feel a sense of relief. In the midst of artificial good cheer and well-meant lies, she seemed to appreciate someone who was willing to be honest. It seemed to free her to be honest herself.

One of the things that distinguishes a genuine artist from a hack is a sense of honesty or integrity. The best painters do not follow slavishly the dictates of their patrons, but express themselves honestly. Pastoral care becomes an art in those moments when we risk being honest in our caring and really engage the person in whose presence we find ourselves.

That engagement requires being "present in the moment." Many of us know the difference between the kind of pastoral call in which we are preoccupied with thoughts about the next thing we are going to do and the kind of encounter where we are fully present to another person. Mentally preparing for a meeting, or emotionally digesting an earlier incident, or just plain fatigue can prevent us from giving people our full attention. What a gift it can be — to us and to the other person — when we can lay aside every other concern and give ourselves wholly to the other. In that kind of encounter, techniques become secondary and pastoral care becomes an art.

That "living in the moment" is something that seems characteristic of Jesus' encounters with people. In his conversations with people in need, there never seems to be a sense that he is wondering whether he remembered to take the roast out of the freezer or worrying about where he is going to spend the night. For the moments that he and another person are together, he gives himself wholly to the other. Certainly Jesus appears as a skilled diagnostician and as a perceptive listener, but it is in the relationships, so quickly established on the trust he inspired, that we see his passion and compassion. It is in them that we see Jesus as artist.

Structuring the Visit

An element of trust is essential if pastoral care is to be an art. If our visits are to be an effective part of our ministry rather than an aimless series of chit-chats, we will need to be intentional about them. Just as a worship service needs to have structure in order to help worshippers move from one "place" at the beginning of the service to another at the end, a pastoral visit needs to have shape if its purpose is to be accomplished in a way that has a sense of art about it.

My colleague, Clair Woodbury wrote an article for pmc magazine a few years ago that suggests the basic structure of a home visit.[3]

Introductions: Take a few minutes to learn people's names, admire their home, get settled in a chair.

Inquiry: Ask how they have been, learn about their extended family, show interest in their work. For people new to the church, an added task is to discover why they have come and what their interests are.

Sharing: Share what is happening at the church, in your life, in the community. Then, last thing, announce you are going to have to leave shortly.

Listening: When you are preparing to leave is often the time when people will reveal their deepest concerns. This is the way we humans are. Herb Cohen, a professional negotiator points out that in negotiating, as in life, "all action occurs at the eleventh hour."[4] You may be saying your goodbye's, but your major task is to be listening very hard. If there is a major concern and you really have to leave, make an appointment right then and there to come back.

These basic components — introductions, inquiry, sharing, listening — are the bare bones of any visit. When the dynamics are well understood, flexibility can be introduced, and you can go on to make each visit a person-to-person encounter that is truly an art-form.

The Place of Prayer

It is not always easy to decide whether or not to offer prayer as part of pastoral care. People may expect a "professional" minister to suggest having a prayer as part of a pastoral visit; in fact, some people may be surprised or even offended if the suggestion is not made. Lay visitors may feel they are on shakier ground and therefore may be more tentative about inviting someone to take part in a prayer together. Whether prayer seems appropriate is often a matter of instinct (art rather than technique). Yet, while many of us would do well to be bolder in asking if people would like to have a prayer, it should never be forced on a person. The suggestion should always be made in a way in which it can be rejected graciously.

When prayer does seem appropriate and those participating feel comfortable, it can add an important dimension to pastoral care. It can remind those taking part that God is involved in the caring. By taking the concerns that have been discussed — or just sensed — and verbalizing them in a prayer celebrating God's presence, the ordinary events of life are uplifted and ennobled. Even when the caregiver is gone, a consciousness of the presence of God will continue.

It can be especially helpful if the person who prays aloud begins with words of thanksgiving. The conversation may have focused mainly on a problem or difficulty, but in every situation there are things for which to be thankful, even if it is only the time two people have been spending together; remembering this can help to put other things into perspective.

In going on to lay before God the concerns that are on the participants' minds, the one offering the prayer can gather up a number of things that may have been discussed. Not only does this bring a sense of order and significance to them, it lets the other person know that he or she has been heard. The prayer, in fact, can provide a catalyst for some unformed thoughts and feelings. It is not uncommon for a prayer to act, not as the final point of a pastoral visit, but as release. Some of us have had the experience of ending a prayer and having the person with us begin to talk again immediately, affirming something that has been said or developing a point in some new direction. Their level of trust in us has been deepened by what they have heard us say, and they have been encouraged to share more.

Little Things

Relationships of trust are rarely cemented in one encounter, yet frequent visits or counselling sessions may not be easy to manage. That's where our understanding of pastoral care needs to be expanded to include other, more fleeting contacts.

A telephone call may not be a substitute for a face-to-face exchange, but it can be a helpful supplement. Just picking up the phone when you think of somebody and checking in on them can be a gesture that has great significance for the person on the other end of the line.

Writing a letter or even a short note can convey a sense of caring that is usually appreciated very much. Clair Woodbury knows of someone who, as a spiritual exercise, developed the habit of writing one thank-you note every day. For this person it brought a realization of how many people he was indebted to — and of his dependence on them and on God. For the recipients of these notes it was often a delightful surprise. They were being thanked more often than not, not for some specific task they had performed, but for what they had come to mean to the writer over the years. It was a gesture that deepened and enhanced many relationships.

Relationships of trust require maintenance if they are to endure. And often it is the little things, the thoughtful gestures, that maintain and build on what has already been established. These, too, are among the things that can elevate pastoral care to an art.

1   Thomas Delbanco, M.D., quoted in Bill Moyers, Healing and the Mind (New York: Doubleday, 1993), p. 23.

2   Thomas Dailey, Address to a Pastoral Care Luncheon, Capital Care Grandview, Edmonton, March 5, 1993.

3   Clair Woodbury, "Ministry as visitation," *pmc* (Winter 1986): 10.

4   Herb Cohen, *You Can Negotiate Anything* (Bantam Books, 1980), p. 92.

Chapter 6

The Art of Leadership

"The first responsibility of a leader is to define reality. The last is to say thank you. In between the two, the leader must become a servant and a debtor. That sums up the progress of an artful leader."

— Max De Pree, *Leadership is an Art*[1]

A tremendous amount has been written in our time on the theory and practice of leadership. The secular world has produced its share. And the church has not neglected the subject. In both spheres people are heard to ask the rhetorical question, "Where's the leadership?"

Where We Have Come From

The church's experience with ministerial leadership has taken a number of interesting turns over the years. Many of us are old enough to remember a time when it was expected that ministers would exercise their leadership in an authoritarian way. The office of minister was held in awe and esteem. The minister was often the best educated person in the congregation. A number of factors combined to place the minister on a pedestal. He — and the masculine pronoun is chosen deliberately — was there to lead, and the people were there to follow. Images of shepherds and sheep were used without any sense of irony.

It was this style of leadership that a friend of mine must have had in mind many years ago when we were travelling in Europe. I had decided that I would begin theological studies when I returned to Canada in the fall. One day apparently, I had offered my friend one piece of advice too many. He turned on me and exploded with the words, "Boy, Saunders, you'll make a *great* minister! You just *love* telling people what to do!"

My friend wasn't the only one who had begun to sense some difficulties with this model of leadership. For one thing, it did not seem to value the ministry of the laity. It was not calculated to enhance the people's sense of ownership of the church's mission and ministry. But, as well, it sometimes led to a "lone ranger" attitude on the part of the ordained minister. At times the minister became the centre of a personality cult that dissolved as soon as he moved on. At other times, an authoritarian style succeeded only in isolating the minister from colleagues and congregation.

A generation or so ago, some congregations began to seek ministers who would relate to them in a different way. Pastoral relations or search committees began to look for staff members who would function as "enablers" or "facilitators" or "animators" or "player-coaches." Many ordained ministers found this approach to be liberating and creative and more cognizant of the idea that clergy and laity are meant to be partners in ministry. In my own denomination, it was a model that appealed particularly to diaconal ministers and had an impact on the church through increasing numbers of people who prepared themselves for diaconal ministry.

In some of its expressions, however, the enabling style of leadership has run into trouble. Sometimes it has amounted almost to an abdication of leadership. If the minister — ordained, diaconal or other — is devoid of ideas and simply waits for people to come and say, "Here's what we want to do; will you help us do it?" the wait may sometimes be a long one. On the other hand, some ministers have learned the language of collegiality, but have used the rhetoric as a substitute for the reality. When one does not acknowledge one's real power and influence, these things may be expressed through manipulation. The enabling style of leadership has not always fulfilled its promise. It is this fact that led consultant Kennon Callahan to conclude as long ago as 1983, "The time for leaders has come; the time for enablers is past."[2]

What shape should leadership take today? Celia Hahn of the Alban Institute sums up our dilemma succinctly when she asks, "Is authority more than 'enablement'? In our confusion many of us find ourselves flipping between two cherished goals that often seem to conflict: we want to take charge and lead courageously, and we want to engage with others in a mutual, collegial way."[3]

We cannot deny the fact that ordered ministers, by virtue of their position, training and experience, generally do have some power and authority and influence. So do church members who occupy positions of leadership on the board or on committees. The question remains — how are power and authority and influence appropriately used? If leadership is an art, how should church leaders express this art? What kind of leadership is appropriate for the times in which we live?

Defining Terms

Before turning to these daunting questions, we find that we have already started to use words in this chapter that require definition. Our definitions are somewhat arbitrary, but some distinctions are necessary if we are to find our way through these sometimes difficult concepts.

Power

I define power as the ability to accomplish ends. Everyone has power. It is something we use every day. Any time we perform a task, any time we accomplish something we use power. Of course, power may not always be used legitimately. We talk about people "throwing their weight around." We know people who use their power to make life difficult for other people. Power can be used to sabotage an enterprise or to manipulate or oppress others. Though we might call power a neutral word, it has negative overtones for many people, especially women. Our experience of power as others have used it may often have been hurtful.

Authority

This word may also provoke a negative reaction — especially when it makes us think of related words like "authoritarian." My understanding of authority, however, is that it means legitimate power. And what makes power legitimate? Well, in some cases it is bestowed on us by others — by an individual or by an organization or by a community. And often the extent of our authority is spelled out in some way. A church board's authority will be spelled out in a manual or constitution. A committee's authority will be detailed in its terms of reference. A staff member's authority may be itemized in a job description.

This kind of authority is often balanced with a list of responsibilities. Job descriptions and terms of reference usually specify not only what authority a person or group has, but what things that authority should be used to accomplish. If both responsibilities and authority are not clearly understood, trouble can easily ensue. When a friend of mine lost his job as minister of a church, his analysis of the situation was that he had been given responsibility to do certain things but denied the authority to carry out his responsibility. By way of contrast, I know of a music director who was unable to fulfill his responsibilities because he was not clear about how much authority he had. When this was spelled out for him, the committee that employed him also saw their need to say, "Use your authority!" In other words, "Use the authority we have given you, and we'll support you in your legitimate use of this power."

In addition to the kind of authority that is formal and that derives from beyond ourselves, there is an informal kind of authority that comes from within. Many of us have had the experience of sitting at a congregational meeting at which some question is debated. The level of the debate may reflect qualities of caution and prudence on the part of the participants. Finally someone stands up to speak — someone who occupies no formal office in the structures of the church at all. Her remarks challenge and shame the rest of us by raising the debate to a whole different level — perhaps by encouraging the congregation to make a faithful decision rather than an expedient one. This person is well-known and well-respected in the church. She may not speak often, but when she does she makes it count. She speaks with moral authority. People pay attention to her not because of the office she holds, but because of the person she is. Many of us have also seen people abuse power at congregational meetings by, in effect, holding the congregation to ransom or by using threats or coercion in an effort to get their way. Their actions may express an illegitimate use of power rather than a use of personal authority.

Sometimes, of course, a person may carry both personal authority and the authority of office. Two chairpersons of the board may have exactly the same authority on paper, but one may need to refer to the authority of office in order to lead. The other may be able to add a greater quality of inner personhood that makes her leadership more effective.

Influence

Another name for personal authority is influence. I once heard of a camp director who was found cleaning out some of the latrines one morning. When someone said that this was no job for the director, he replied, "I can't ask someone to do something I'm not prepared to do myself." Rather than relying on the authority of his office, the director chose to lead by example and trust that his example would influence the attitudes of the campers.

That, really, was the way Jesus went about it in the upper room. When he took on the role of a slave, a position with virtually no power or authority in itself, and washed the disciples' feet, he was using his personal authority to set an example — an example that would influence the future attitudes and behaviour of the disciples.[4]

Effective leaders know how to use whatever authority has been bestowed on them by others as well as the authority of their own persons.

Management and leadership

These two terms need to be defined before we look at how authority can be used. Most writers on leadership take care to distinguish between management and leadership. Managers concentrate on administration. They tend to assume that both human and material resources are finite and that the best one can do is arrange them in efficient patterns. Managers may set goals, but the goals tend to be earthbound and short-term. Leaders, on the other hand, are inspired by a larger vision — one that is not limited by the apparent realities of the moment.

In a variation on this distinction, leadership theorist James McGregor Burns used the terms "transactors" and "transformers."[5] Of transacting leaders, what I would call managers, Baptist teacher Robert D. Dale says that they

> ... simply allot resources according to exchanges. They practice the art of compromise or *quid pro quo*, trading "something for something." Transactors are traders and bargainers. But the bargain is an end in itself. Beyond the bargain, there's no enduring purpose or vision holding the leader and follower together.
>
> On the other hand, "transforming leaders" elevate, envision, mobilize, inspire, exalt, uplift, and exhort. The power of a common vision and the intensity of the engagement binds leaders and followers together for the future.[6] Transformational leadership has a moral dimension because it ultimately "raises the level of human conduct and ethical aspiration of both leader and led, and thus it has a transforming effect on both."[7]

Transformational leadership, in other words, is leadership with a message. That is one of the things that makes it art.

Burns, Dale and others return again and again to the idea that one of the things that distinguishes leadership from management is vision. Vision is the quality that imagines what an institution — like a church — can be. It is vision that enables leaders to fulfill what Max De Pree calls the first responsibility of a leader, namely "to define reality."[8]

For many of us, vision is a scary word. It evokes images of going into a kind of trance until some picture becomes clear to us. But vision for the future is rarely discontiguous with what has gone before. Often it involves the generating of ideas about how a congregation can develop itself further and in a way that more fully lives out its mission and its purpose. Ministers sometimes feel burdened by the sense that they are the only people in the congregation who are expected to have vision. Really, the transforming leaders in any congregation are those who can get beyond the nuts and bolts of day-to-day management to imagine together where that church might go and what it might yet become.

Unlike managers (transactors) whose values are survival and maintenance and keeping everybody together, transforming leaders are willing to take risks for the sake of the vision, the thing to which God is calling this community of faith. For ministers, the idea of transaction may appeal to the pastor in them (the person caring for persons), while the idea of transformation appeals to the prophet (the person who hears and articulates the call of God).

Having described some leadership styles that we have seen in the past and having defined some terms, let's turn to some of the things that make for effective leadership today.

Effective Leadership

We hear a lot these days about "leadership styles." Every writer in the field seems to have his or her own method of categorizing the ways in which we give leadership — as well as their own questionnaires to help us discover what our leadership style is. Some contrast "task-oriented" with "people-oriented" styles. George D. Parsons' "PACE Profile" is designed to rate our relative strengths in terms of Predicting, Attending, Conducting and Excelling styles. Robert Dale talks about catalysts, encouragers, commanders and hermits. Celia Hahn identifies the exercise of four kinds of authority: received, autonomous, assertive and integrated. And so it goes.

We sometimes get the impression that each of us has only one leadership style and that, whether it's good or bad, we're stuck with it. At best, we may learn from some books on leadership that we have a "preferred" style and that we have other styles to fall back on when we feel threatened or our preferred style doesn't work. More and more we are discovering that effective leaders need to be flexible; they need to be able to size up a situation and bring to it the appropriate kind of leadership.

Working with a committee that is highly motivated but has as yet little understanding of its responsibilities, the leader (chairperson or staff member) may need to be very directive. Where a group is more experienced and has a clear sense of what it is about, a more passive leadership style — being available for advice and consultation — may be all that is needed. A church board that is highly skilled and competent, but that cannot see beyond management issues, may need a leader to help them to "see visions and dream dreams."

Given that situations vary, that different people in a congregation have different expectations of their leaders, and that even the same congregational member may have one set of expectations on Monday and a different set on Tuesday, means that effective leadership requires insight and flexibility. Norman Shawchuck calls this quality "adaptive leadership."[9] Paul Hersey and Kenneth H. Blanchard coined (and registered!) the term "Situational Leadership" to suggest somewhat the same thing.[10] To be able to recognize what kind of leadership is needed in a particular situation requires experience and intuition. In other words, there is an art to it. It is this art that Shawchuck is describing when he writes:

> In order to be fully effective a leader must develop two important skills: the ability to employ a variety of leadership behaviors and the ability to determine which set of behaviors would be most effective with a particular group at a given point in time. Stated another way, a leader must be able to match the most appropriate leadership style to the group's level of ability to perform a given task.[11]

What else does effective leadership require? As with other art forms we have identified in other chapters, it requires both a message and a sensitivity to the audience to which the message is directed. We have already described the message in terms of "vision" — bringing some sense of how things ought to be. Unlike some artists who produce their work and set it up and say, "There it is," leaders are constantly interacting with other people. If they want to be effective in the way they introduce an idea, they need to understand the "audience" because this is an audience that will affect the message. It is important, therefore, to know where the people are and to begin there. It is important to understand how people may be threatened by the possibility of change and to work with rather than against them. It is important to recognize people's need for ownership of an idea and for the leader not to be so invested in the vision that s/he cannot let go of it and allow the community to work on it, adapting and shaping it, changing it and making it their own. In these and many other ways, effective leaders need not only some convictions about "vision," but some understanding of the human setting in which the vision will take on life. With that understanding, leaders will have an essential tool for "adaptive leadership."

In identifying some of the requirements for effective leadership, more needs to be said about the message. If you are the leader and you do, indeed, have some ideas about where you would like to see the institution (in this case, the church) going, how do you deal with reactions of hostility or indifference? How do you deal with those whose ideas may be different? Do you capitulate? Do you become defensive or aggressive? Do you fall victim to the varied expectations and projections of members of the congregation, trying vainly to satisfy everyone? Do you decide that peace is more important than vision and revert to the role of pouring oil on troubled waters? Do you vacillate between one form of behaviour and another and confuse everyone with your mixed signals? At a deeper level, how do you feel? Rejected? Threatened? Abandoned? Misunderstood? Do you become so caught up in other people's feelings and reactions that you don't really know how you feel?

More and more writers are concluding that, of the factors that make for effective leadership, one that cannot be ignored is the interior life of the leader. Leaders need to have a well-developed sense of self-awareness and, if possible, of self-acceptance. They need these things, not so that they can exude an inflexible, stick-to-your-guns kind of self-confidence. Quite the contrary. They need them so that they can offer appropriate and flexible leadership with a sense of inner security and integrity. To put it negatively, it is difficult to lead effectively if you do not know yourself, if you always have something to prove, if you cannot laugh at your mistakes, or if your ego is so fragile it will crumble at a touch.

None of us comes to a position of leadership without acquiring a psycho-spiritual history that imposes limits on our ability either to know or to accept ourselves. Growth in these areas is a spiritual journey, but there are companions available for us. There are resources that can help us along the way. Prayer and meditation are among them. So is the practice of keeping a journal — reflecting in writing on our experiences and insights. So is a circle of trusted friends who are able to offer us constructive criticism in an atmosphere of care and support. Some of us have turned to counsellors or consultants, to therapists or spiritual directors. Each of these people serves a different purpose and we may require help in identifying what it is we need at this particular stage of our lives. In any case, few of us can come to know ourselves well in isolation. And few of us can become convinced of our acceptability without sensing God's love for us mediated through some human agent.

Effective leaders are people who not only know what to do. They also know how to be — or at least they are in the process of learning. In art, the message comes from within. Leaders are artists who need to have some sense of the inner person from whom their leadership comes.

No doubt there are many other requirements for effective leadership. Here we will list just one more, a very simple one: time. Whether you are a staff member or a member of a board or committee, you will know that it takes time for visions to be realized. That is what makes it so important for ministers and other leaders to sign on for the long haul.

A minister I know has a pattern of serving a congregation for two or three years and then moving on. He is full of energy and ideas and deeply committed to social action. But I suspect that, from the point of view of the congregations he has served, he is a one-man band: someone who roars into town, lays out all his convictions, stirs things up, campaigns (pretty much on his own) for some causes, and then moves on. And the congregation, after catching its breath, returns to business as usual. They are not changed or transformed because they have not felt valued. And they have not felt valued because their minister has not stayed long enough to get to know them, to listen to their concerns, to engage them and work with them in getting from "A" to "B." In other words, he has not given the time it takes to be an effective leader.

In the same way, many of us know people who have agreed to give leadership to a board or committee, but who do not take the time to understand where the group has come from. They serve a two-year term and then disappear into the woodwork again — to be succeeded, perhaps, by someone else who doesn't take time to find out what vision-making was in process, but who sets off again in a very different direction. There are few things more frustrating to followers than a "stop-start" approach to leadership. Church members should not have to ask, "Well, what's it going to be today?" They need leaders — and a continuity of leaders — who share a vision they can articulate, to which they are prepared to give the time required for gestation. If it is true that *effective* leaders are *trusted* leaders, time must be given to allow trust to grow.

Thoughts for the Church Board

Because of the disproportionate amount of leadership literature that is directed toward ministers, we sometimes get the impression that ministers are the leaders and the laity are the led. It does not have to be so. In fact, it is not healthy for it to be so. If it is the task of leaders to "define reality" and to capture visions and to articulate the purpose of the group, then this needs to be a shared enterprise. Church boards in particular need to see themselves as the body that leads the congregation, as leaders rather than merely managers, as transformers rather than merely transactors.

It was with a view to clarifying its leadership role that the Board of the church where I serve embarked on a process that included a day with Clair Woodbury and Joyce Madsen of the Canadian Centre for Congregational Life. If it is true that individual leaders need a sense of self-awareness in order to lead effectively, we felt that a sense of self-awareness was important for us as a group if the Board was to lead effectively.

We began to realize that we had not done enough to help Board members see one another as people rather than simply as decision-makers. We sensed that if we knew one another better, understood something of one another's background and convictions, it would help us to understand the perspectives that each person brought to the Board's discussions. And so we became more intentional about including in our meetings opportunities for interaction and socializing on a personal level. We began to hold annual retreats and orientations at which Board members had an opportunity to tell stories about how they came to be a part of this congregation and to express their feelings about the church.

Then we had a sense that we needed to define — more succinctly than any constitution or terms of reference might do — what the Board was really about. Initially we found it easier to define what the Board did not and should not do than to identify what it does and should do. Eventually, however, we found that we could gather our Board's authority and responsibility under four headings: vision, policy, communications, and finance. The Board, we said, is the body that defines the congregation's vision, its sense of what it is and of where it should be going. In broad terms, it is the body that sets policy for the congregation, policy that is consistent with our sense of vision. The Board has responsibility for communicating, both between the Board and its committees and between the Board and the congregation. And, although there are committees to deal with the day-to-day raising and spending of money, the Board has ultimate responsibility from one annual meeting to the next for the financial well-being of the institution and is accountable to God and to the congregation for their stewardship of that responsibility.

Having defined our areas of authority and responsibility, we began to find it easier to monitor and police our actions at Board meetings. Sometimes by means of a formal review at the end of the meeting, and sometimes by increased self-awareness as we went along, we would try to ensure that we hadn't strayed too much into detail when we had defined our job as seeing the bigger picture, that we hadn't done a committee's work over again when their authority in a particular area was clearly spelled out, that we didn't become preoccupied with management rather than leadership, that we weren't concentrating on means rather than ends, that we didn't assign a task and then look over people's shoulders as they performed it.

As a minister on staff, I was interested to see how my own leadership style began to shift as we went through this process. A role that staff may always be required to play is that of providing information. As the people who work for the institution day by day, staff members are the people to whom the volunteers may legitimately turn for information so that their decisions may be informed ones. Nevertheless, in my earlier years at the church, I found myself going home from meeting after meeting feeling that I had said too much, spoken to too many issues, expressed too many opinions.

With these new developments, I found that I was saying more about process and less about substance and outcomes. In other words, my leadership role and style were shifting. In the early stages of the shift, I was often the one who would say, "I think we may have defined the issue sufficiently and have a sense of direction about it; now we're starting to do the work of the Stewardship Committee. Maybe it's time to refer the detailed work to the appropriate group." As time went on, others began to share more and more in the task of "self-monitoring" and of checking what we were doing against the four general areas in which we had defined our authority and responsibility. As well, increasingly I found myself raising questions about the values behind an issue and challenging the Board to keep these values in mind in their decision-making.

We also began to see the need for the Board to be made up of people who were prepared to work at providing leadership rather than management — people with vision, people who had ideas about policy. And for the health of the organization we saw the need for a Board with a spectrum of opinion that was neither too broad nor too narrow. If the range of beliefs and values held by the members of a governing body are too broad, it may be difficult to find consensus on significant issues. The collection of generally held convictions may be so small that every substantive matter will provoke extensive debate, and the group will find that decisions can only be made by majority vote — a situation that creates winners and losers. In such a situation it may be difficult to agree on a shared vision, on appropriate policy, on how to define reality. In short it may be difficult for the Board to lead.

If, on the other hand, the range of shared assumptions is too narrow the Board may lose its capacity to be self-critical. Some of us have had the experience of joining a group where a common set of values seems to be assumed by everyone. If we have been inclined to question some of these values, we may have found that our questions have not been welcomed. We may have learned that our presence is appreciated only if we share — or pretend to share — the beliefs and prejudices of the group. We may feel that we don't belong and choose to leave. Or we may decide that non-conformity is not worth the strain, and simply go along with the others. Either way the group loses. It is important for a church Board to be self-aware, to have a sense of what it is and what it is about. Though a Board should resist attempts to derail or sabotage its efforts, to be healthy it needs to be able to hear those who challenge assumptions it takes for granted. It is good for a Board to have on it a few people who have the skill and the courage to do that, who are not content simply to "toe the party line." Their role is to keep the leadership honest, to help Board members challenge one another to justify their decisions and the convictions on which they are based.

The potential for church boards to exercise genuine leadership is enormous. Sadly, too many boards busy themselves with the detailed work of management. Or they bemoan changes in circumstances rather than being alert to new challenges. Or they leave the leadership entirely to the professional staff — at least until a staff member makes a decision with which the board disagrees. When boards take seriously their responsibility to share with the staff in the art of leadership, board meetings can cease to be tedious and can become significant events; boards can be transformed from reactive to pro-active bodies and the church can be given the leadership it needs and deserves.

1   Max De Pree, *Leadership is an Art* (New York: Dell Publishing, 1989), p. 11.

2   Kennon Callahan, *Twelve Keys to an Effective Church* (San Francisco: Harper & Row, 1983), p. 41.

3   Celia Allison Hahn, *Growing in Authority: Relinquishing Control* (Washington: Alban Institute, 1994), p. 4.

4   See John 13:3–17.

5   James McGregor Burns, *Leadership* (New York: Harper and Row, 1978).

6   Robert D. Dale, *Good News for Great Leaders* (Washington: Alban Institute, 1992).

7   Burns, p. 20.

8   De Pree, p. 11.

9   Norman Shawchuck, *How To Be A More Effective Church Leader* (Leith, North Dakota: Spiritual Growth Resources, 1990).

10   Paul Hersey and Kenneth H. Blanchard, *Situational Leadership: A Summary* (Leadership Studies, Inc., 1976).

11   Shawchuck, p.33.

Part II

Clair Woodbury

Introduction

The role of the artist is exactly the same as the role of the lover.
If I love you, I have to make you conscious of the things
you don't see.

— James Baldwin[1]

$\mathcal{I}$ grew up in a home where art was all around me. My father was a professional musician and amateur painter. Our walls were hung with crashing waves, autumn leaves, simmering Cairo streets and portraits of famous composers. Evenings were filled with Chopin études and piano students pounding out the results of a week of practice.

When I went into the church as a professional I brought my love of art and artistry with me. I knew from years of piano lessons that for music to become an art you had to learn the basic techniques, practice to develop your skill, listen until the music began to speak to you, then add that unknown element that made your playing an expression of your own personality as well as the composer's thought.

I have always enjoyed writing. Shaping words until they convey just what you want to communicate has been a very satisfying challenge. I remember when speaking in public became an art. I had returned to the pastorate after ten years in community development. Each week I wrote out my sermon and polished the words until they shone. I more or less read the manuscripts on Sunday morning from the pulpit. I admit I had fallen in love with my words.

The chair of our Board, Bill Ziegler, was a feisty former Brigadier in the Canadian Army, retired CEO of a large company. He invited me to his home for a chat. Half way through the visit he got to the heart of the matter. "When are you going to get your nose out of your notes and talk to us?" Public speaking, he said, is an art, and proceeded to give me a step-by-step lecture on how to do it. It was the most helpful class I ever attended. Speaking without notes meant extra work. But if I couldn't remember what I was going to say, Bill had told me, how could I expect anyone in the congregation to remember. Leaving the manuscript behind provided a great freedom to observe how people were responding, to speak directly from the heart, to become more one with my message and with those I was addressing. I knew what the Jewish novelist Elie Wiesel meant when he wrote, "The more I am able to write out of my Jewishness, the more universally I am able to communicate."

When developed to the point where it is an art, the spoken word is quite different from written communication. In the same way, each ministry — no matter what it might be — is different from the others. Each has its skills to develop, its own language to learn, and its own way of becoming an expression of who I am and what I want to communicate.

I want to emphasize that ministry is something that takes place at work, in the home, with colleagues on the golf course, at the pottery workshop, in the choral society. If the spirit of Christ is guiding our life, then Christian ethics determine relationships at work, Christ-like love dominates our contribution at home, Christian caring and sharing emerge as we play and be together.

This second part of our book deals with innovation in the church, but also with artful ways to innovate in the workplace. It deals with management in the home, managing conflict wherever it emerges, encouraging whomever whenever however. It deals with giving, not just till it hurts, but until it helps spiritually. It talks about loyalty to team-mates, with whomever you are working or living. Most important, it talks about staying in love with God, because without that particular art, these other ministries remain a medium without a message.

People seem so stressed out these days, so busy. It is possible to become so preoccupied with providing, procuring and preparing for life that one never gets around to actually living life. This section is about being "really alive" to all of life's opportunities and joys, as well as to life's challenges.

1.   James Baldwin, quoted in Isabel Carter Heyword, *The Redemption of God* (New York: University Press of America, 1982), p. 217.

Chapter 7

The Art of Innovation

Wherever I found new churches growing and older churches being re-vitalized, and special ministries being carried out with intensity, I found members of the Order of Ministry and lay people who are entrepreneurs, dreamers, idea people, innovators, people who have the ability to turn their dreams into action.

— Brian Aitkin, based on cross-Canada research[1]

The information age is transforming the world, and a very secular world is issuing a challenge to which the church must respond if it is to remain an effective instrument for communicating God's Good News. Loren Mead of the Alban Institute observes the church has "slipped off the radar screen" for a large number of people.[2] What has happened?

There are four major shifts that are taking place in the way the church relates to society. They have to do with the relationship of Christians to the community, to other faiths, to themselves and to God. Innovation is required at the theological level to express our new understanding of who we are and how we relate to God. At the same time, congregations face the week-by-week challenge of integrating new people into their fellowship. There is a constant requirement to introduce new programs for these new people. The art of innovation is what this chapter is all about.[3]

Community

When I was growing up, people generally acknowledged the importance of the church, even if a considerable number did not actually attend regularly. Church was a place to be seen if you wanted to get ahead in business or be considered a solid citizen. Now the mention of where you were on Sunday tends to draw the comment, "You still go to church?"

Schools were partners in Christian education. My grade seven teacher, for example, read us the whole Gospel of John and gave us all copies. Today it is no longer possible for a school teacher to advocate the Christian faith in a classroom that contains as many Muslims, Hindus, and Buddhists as practicing Christians.

Main-line churches welcomed any child for baptism. Though the child's parents might not be church members, we could assume that children were at the very least under the influence of a society that acknowledged Christian values. Churches now find they need to introduce baptismal courses for parents who have little or no knowledge of what it means to produce a Christian environment in the home.

It is certainly true that many of the values people hold are basically secular. There is a self-centredness that is wide-spread, a me-first attitude that puts the maintenance of First World wealth ahead of world-wide well-being. Church attendance has declined. Those who do attend are more selective and do much more shopping around before choosing a congregation, and think little of crossing denominational lines if the congregation feels right. Those who seek to plant churches in new neighbourhoods are no longer welcomed but are confronted with petitions from angry residents complaining that the increased traffic will endanger their children and shatter the peace of their Sunday morning. What is going on?

The clues can be found in the changed attitudes of the so-called Baby Boom generation, those born between 1945 and 1962. Examine the following list carefully, and see if it is not so much Christianity that is being rejected as the institutional church.

- **Space:** People today expect more space in their homes and their public buildings, and are unwilling to put up with cramped quarters or clutter. Many churches, however, excel in clutter.
- **Cleanliness:** People have high standards for cleanliness in public facilities — especially the nursery, kitchen, entrance, etc. Older churches are often musty smelling and cut corners on janitorial service.
- **Risk:** Congregations used to wait until increased numbers justified adding staff or increasing the building size. People today know you have to add staff and space first in order to grow. It's a "build it and they will come" attitude. Operating out of safety has given way to the need for risk.

- **Service:** People are willing to pay for quality service. Their willingness to fund institutions like the church is more linked to the level of service provided than to the concept of giving to God.
- **Involvement:** People today want a way to give themselves in compassion. They want personal involvement, not just to give money.
- **Event:** Events more than ideas are what stick in people's minds.
- **Practical:** People are pragmatic. They want it to work. Results are more important than beliefs.
- **Spiritual:** Institutional loyalty may be in decline, but all the evidence indicates a deep spirituality and sensitivity to soul.
- **Now:** Pie in the sky when you die? Forget it. Instant gratification is in.
- **Environment:** Young people are exhibiting a sensitivity and a care for the environment that rivals the evangelical fervour of a previous age.

Those are the top ten changes I see. When I look at them, it is not so much the basic concepts of Christianity that are being questioned as the cultural practices or the plain sloppiness of the traditional church. I go into many church buildings that are dark, deteriorating and even dirty. That's not the type of house I live in, nor the standard of public building I will accept. I am used to high quality service at the supermarket, from my car dealer, in my entertainment. Church shoppers report quality is hard to find.

Another issue is the intense interest today in spirituality, yet the church seems to be the last place they look. Loren Mead, former director of the Alban Institute, observes:

> Ordinary people who have extraordinary spiritual experiences often do not think that their congregations or clergy would be interested in or able to help interpret such experiences. It is as if people have separated deep personal religious experience from congregational life. They feel that the congregation expect their support and attendance at worship and activities, but that the congregation has no interest in their religious experience."[4]

Businesses go out of business when sales figures become more important than meeting customer needs. This is the clue to where innovation needs to take place, in developing the programs and approaches that match current needs and values.

Other Faiths

We have gone through a whole series of shifts in the way we view other faiths. For the first half of this century, so-called Christian countries viewed the rest of the world as the mission field. The 60's saw a romanticizing of other religions. Indian gurus invaded North America, and no university campus was complete without a comparative religion department. Then came the waves of immigration. We found Buddhists, Muslims and Hindus living beside us, leading Scout groups, raising funds for the community league.

Today we live in a pluralistic society that has made a place for neighbours who are new to North America. This pluralism has become a deep challenge to the church's understanding of itself. If other faiths are to be respected, what is unique about the Christian faith? Is Christianity just one religion among many, as good or as bad as any other? We find we increasingly have to distinguish between "good religion" and "bad religion," between good Christianity and Christianity badly practiced. The challenge is to develop criteria we can use in making these judgments.

Ourselves

There has been a shift in the way we understand basic human nature. Since the time of Augustine in the 5th century, the Christian church has operated out of a doctrine of original sin. Human beings were at heart pernicious, and only Christian baptism could remove that tendency.

That view was challenged first in the school system by the likes of John Dewey. Children are essentially good and want to grow. Removing the obstacles to that growth is what education is about. This approach began to find its way into Sunday School curricula. For fifty years, Sunday Schools operated out of a theology of "original blessing," while in the sanctuary the preaching was based on original sin. It is a schizophrenia that could not last forever.

In the days of full blown original sin, clergy were assumed to have a little less of it than ordinary people. They needed to be up front when talking to

God. In congregations that lean toward original blessing, there has been a shift from "let the clergy do it" to a recognition that lay people have a true ministry. Innovating ways to enable and recognize that ministry is the challenge.

Our Image of God

There has been a shift in our understanding of God from one who intervenes to one who empowers us. When I was growing up, we still paid lip service to the intervening God, but did not really expect very much. The classic story is of the church service where the farming community came to pray for rain, but the preacher noticed no one had brought an umbrella.

Four decades ago J. B. Phillips told the church of the '50s *Your God is Too Small*. The picture the church was painting of God (distant tyrant, strict parent, religious policeman, or "Santa-Claus-in-the-sky") was too small to contain people's religious experience. A world-wide movement took place that resulted in a more adequate picture of God. Voices are telling us that once again our concept of God is too small. For example, Desmond Tutu, the South African Bishop who has come to symbolize the church's opposition to apartheid, described for *Life Magazine* an image of God that is a radical departure from the traditional:

> I am not a pacifist, like Martin Luther King or Mahatma Gandhi. I couldn't stand by and see someone throw children into a gas chamber. How could God allow that? How could God make obviously evil people succeed against children? Ultimately, all you can say is that God does not occupy an Olympian vastness, remote from us. God has this deep, deep solidarity with us. God became a human being, a baby. God was hungry. God was tired. God suffered and died. God is there with us.[5]

This is a time of energizing opportunity. A time for innovation on a grand scale. We need an enlarged picture of God, one grand enough to contain all our diverse experiences of God. We need a deeper understanding of ourselves as the complex mixture of good and evil that we are. We need to develop criteria that will help us distinguish good religion from bad religion, criteria that can be applied to the practice of Christianity as well as the practice of Buddhism, Islam and all the other religions of the world. We need a new understanding of what it means to be the church in an increasingly secular society.

Now let's turn to the innovation required at a more practical level, the creation of new groups as entry points into congregations.

The Church as a Bakery

My wife and I lived for two years in a small Italian mountain village, volunteer participants in an economic renewal process. We started a preschool, organized neighbourhood meetings, located seed grain for farmers. Our carpentry shop began making copies of the traditional *casa panca* or bread chest. Assembled with no nails, only wooden pegs, and made of birch, it held a dozen or so round Italian loaves. In the early days, families baked only once a week in the village beehive oven. The bread was stored in these bread-chests. Though it developed a very hard crust and took a sharp knife to cut, it nourished the family well for the whole week.

Church groups are like those loaves of bread. Over time they develop a hard crust, which makes it very difficult for new people to get in. It is not that the members of established groups have bad intentions or are unfriendly. It is simply that most folks lead busy lives and have room for only so many relationships. Once in a group, they establish friendships, become accustomed to each other, develop memories, rehearse a common history. The crust thickens.[6]

New people are best served by new loaves (groups where the crust has not yet developed). New people have room for new friendships. They can make room in their lives for others.

We were newly arrived in Rome. We had nine months to learn Italian and help locate a village that would welcome a development project. Our heads were spinning with the new culture, new language, and the bureaucratic challenge of trying to enroll two young boys in Italian schools. It was our second or third Sunday at Rome Methodist Church that we met Paul and Ruth. They were new to the city too, fresh from a United Nations fish culture project in what was then Yugoslavia. We walked home from church together, the beginning of a friendship that has lasted to this day.

Consultants working with congregations stress the importance of new groups for new people. For Kennon Callahan, launching new groups is one of his twelve keys to an effective congregation.[7] His United States experience indicated the magic number was one new group for every 20 new people. Canadians are a bit more reserved and are not quite as group-oriented as Americans. In Canada, I would recommend launching a new group for every 30 new people who become part your congregation.

By new people, we are not just talking about people new to the community. We include people entering a new phase of life. People recently separated or divorced usually find they need to locate a whole new set of friends. People change as they move through the years and need new groups where they can meet with similar interests. Some people need Bible study at a certain phase in their life, others spiritual exercises, others experience in the practice of prayer, others an improved social life, others just a group where they can talk things over. Many are looking for a group that will help them to be of service to other people, a way of giving themselves in compassion.

When I was growing up, the church was in the industrial age. National programmes promoted groups that were exactly the same in every congregation. Women's groups, men's groups, youth groups, Canadian Girls in Training, the troops and packs of the Scouting movement — all came with organizational manuals and recommended structures. We now live in the information age. It is individual identity rather than community conformity that strongly motivates our living and buying habits. Whether clothing, careers or cars, we want what we wear and drive to say who we are, to make a statement. The same is true of the programmes in which we participate. Whatever it is, it has to fit our needs.

Here are some of the ways to launch new groups.

The Teamed Leadership Model

Church staff have a special responsibility for integrating new people. When they notice an area of special interest to several people, the staff person locates another person in the congregation willing to work with them as a team leader. People who are new to the congregation are given a personal invitation to become part of the group. After a month or so, the two leaders look for someone from the group who is willing to be part of the leadership team. When that happens, the staff person steps aside in order to begin the process with the new people who have arrived in the meantime.

Leadership Training Model

In this model, a group of potential leaders are recruited for specific training in a process they will then facilitate for others. There are a number of six or eight week Bible study programmes based on this model. It can also be used for training in pastoral care, or in developing skill in any number of areas in a congregation. The initial group goes through the six or eight week training, then individually or in pairs they lead a group of their own. While the initial group of leaders is in training, expectations are raised within the congregation and the second round of participants recruited. If the congregation is large enough and interest sufficient, a third round may be possible.

Dinner Party Model

In this model, members of the congregation who could potentially become a group are identified, either by staff or by a lay leader. It may be a cluster of individuals who are new to the congregation. It may be a group identifiable by lifestyle or age — singles, young adults, seniors. It may be a group with a particular need. All those who have been identified are given an invitation to a special event, usually involving a meal. The invitation clearly specifies the affinity area. "We are inviting all young adults..." "We are inviting all seniors who are new to the congregation..." "We are inviting everyone who has expressed an interest in forming a Bible study group..." Dinner and an opportunity to get to know one another is followed by an open discussion as to whether people are interested in meeting regularly, and what that would look like. Sometimes nothing happens, and it was just a good get-together. Sometimes leadership emerges immediately out of the group and a new "loaf" is up and running. Sometimes staff have to provide leadership until the group gets established.

Community Partnership Model

There are many agencies and organizations in most communities who welcome congregations as partners: women's shelters, senior's centres, friendship houses, inner-city centres, literacy centres, schools, correctional institutions, prisons. Schools need grandparents to read to children. A congregation can supply breakfasts or lunches for children from families in poverty situations. Shelters need equipment and people to act as hosts or do friendship counseling. The list of needs goes on and on. This approach can give people who want to be helpful but don't know where to start, a way of becoming involved. A congregation that picks one or two of these community organizations can find that the work not only is helpful to the organizations, but the project releases energy and creates ways for people to bond together in the congregation.

"Initiative around a Need" Model

A phone call arrives late one night from the national office: "We have a refugee that needs a sponsoring congregation. Can you help?" Visitors contact a new family in the community, and discover the husband has just been released from prison and needs help locating a job. Two friends, both of whom have been laid off and are going through the process of seeking employment, wonder how many other people in the congregation are in the same situation. People from a congregation notice the number of seniors' residences being built in their community, and wonder if there is a need for a seniors' programme in their church. All these "calls" invite an initiative to meet a specific need in the community or in the congregation. This model has congregational leadership — both lay and staff — on the lookout for special needs, and ready to mobilize the congregation's resources to respond to those needs. It is an approach that takes sensitivity, and imagination, as every need is different.

The "Loafers" Model

There are a number of programs specifically designed to develop small groups within a congregation. One is the "Mariners" program. People sign up for passage on various "ships" in the congregation's fleet. Ships contain couples or singles, some as many as 25 people, most smaller, and meet in members' homes. At monthly meetings of each ship, the host plans the activities — sometimes social activities such as dinner, bowling, or Thanksgiving celebration — sometimes Bible study, a special speaker, a Seder meal. Ships with parents include their children in some activities — a picnic, roller-skating, summer camping. Every ship carries some cargo, a work project for the church such as painting a classroom, repairing a senior's fence, or weeding the church garden. One ship could play the handy-repair role in the congregation. Fleet admirals and ship skippers constitute the Skippers' Council that meets quarterly to coordinate fleet-wide projects. Staff play a special role in inviting newcomers or those with a common interest to be part of a new ship.[8]

Characteristics of an Entrepreneur

A great deal of research has been done on the characteristics of entrepreneurs who are good at initiating new groups. Entrepreneurs tend to be self-starters with an abundance of energy. Are they born or are they made? Barrie

Day of Edmonton's Career Development Institute says, "I believe entrepreneurship can be taught. Behaviours can be learned."[9]

Successful entrepreneurs are motivated by a challenge. They tend to seek out expert advice when they encounter a difficult situation, rather than trying to muddle through on their own. Church entrepreneurs believe religious service is a partnership with God that requires skill and hard work on their part. They are willing to risk, but only after carefully considering the options and chances for success.

As far as personality traits are concerned, starters tend to be persistent, self-confident, well-organized — people who have a positive outlook on life and are optimistic about the future of the church.

In the secular world, no one would think of launching an enterprise without a well-documented business plan. The successful church entrepreneur is equally diligent about developing a careful plan before launching a new group or initiative in a congregation. Jesus did have a parable about making a careful assessment before beginning to build. Normally a plan would include the following:

- an assessment of the leadership that is available for the initiative
- a clear description of the idea
- an assessment of the need and the likely response
- the physical facilities required by the initiative
- the financial resources the initiative will require, together with an estimate of the resources it may eventually generate.

Innovation as an Art

There are principles that can be learned for launching new groups:
- The invitation to join should be personal, should demonstrate quality, and should supply a full picture.
- It is important to push for a critical mass, an initial group large enough to give people the feeling that they have the support of like-minded people.
- Trained leadership is key to group success.
- Once techniques have been mastered, the development of innovation as an art can begin:
- Listening for the real needs of people below what they say are their needs is an art that has to be developed. For someone who is alert, a phrase overheard in the coffee line or in the office can reveal a new opportunity.

- Creating the confidence of a group in your ability as a leader can be an art. So is being able to step back in a way that lets new leadership emerge from a group.
- Every new initiative will encounter some resistance. The ability to ensure the backing of the establishment is a political art that cannot be neglected.

When it comes to innovation in the area of theology (our understanding of how we relate to God and to each other) that challenge is much greater. We once left that kind of work to professors in theological colleges. The world is changing too fast and has become too specialized. Each new situation demands that we rethink what is the right thing to do, the ethical thing to do, the loving thing to do. The questions are the same: "What is the just thing to do?" "What is the truly caring thing to do?" "What would Jesus do?" Depending on the situation, the answers can be very different. Innovation is the art of thinking through all the approaches, even trying them one by one, until the approach that is truly right reveals itself. That is the art of discovering God's will, the art of theological innovation.

1   Brian Aitkin, *Theological Education in the 80's* (The United Church of Canada, 1988).

2   Loren Mead, *Transforming Congregations for the Future* (Washington: The Alban Institute, 1994).

3   For further reading: Donald P. Smith, *How to Attract and Keep Active Church Members* (Louisille: Westminster/John Knox Press, 1992). This book, based on research in six hundred congregations, contains a multitude of ideas for programs and initiatives.

4   Loren Mead, p. 53.

5   Archbishop Desmond Tutu, *Life Magazine* (December, 1990), p.49.

6   Our thanks to George Parsons, Alban Institute consultant, for the analogy of the congregation as a bakery.

7   Kennon Callahan, *Twelve Keys to an Effective Congregation* (new York: Harper + Row, 1983), p. 35.

8   The Mariner Program is described in: Donald P. Smith, *How to Attract and Keep Active Church Members* (Louisville: Westminster/John Knox Press, 1992).

9   *Are You Cut Out to be an Entrepreneur?* (Alberta Career Development and Employment, 1988), p. 7.

Chapter 8

The Art of Management

By organizational effectiveness we mean the capacity of the organization to be responsive and adaptive to its environment.

— Michael Beer, Harvard Business School[1]

Dorothy Mundle was my partner in ministry for five years. I knew when she was due to arrive in the office because the phone calls would start to come in for her. She would have been on the phone from her home, setting up meetings, checking with group leaders, leaving messages if people were not available, and talking to people who knew that first thing in the morning was a good time to catch her. When they could not reach her at home, they would try the office. That's how we knew she was in her car on the way.

When she did arrive, more often than not, she would spend the first ten minutes standing at her desk, still wearing her coat, on the phone. Someone had called just as she walked in, or while she was on the way she had thought of someone she needed to phone.

Telephone management is a great way to keep in touch with people, support them and let them know their contribution is valued. My favourite piece of management equipment was the computer. My first task in the morning was to turn it on. I used it to design visitation districts, send notes, create committee job descriptions, assemble worship services. Providing good clear guidelines was my contribution to supporting our visitors, committee members and worship leaders.

I learned from Dorothy the value of the telephone to keep in touch with people, and use the phone a lot more now. Dorothy learned from me the power of the computer to convey information.

Management is an art, which means there is no one way of doing it. The parade of management techniques in the business world includes Management Grid Training, Management by Objectives, Quality of Work Life, Survey Feedback, Sensitivity Groups and Team Building. A Harvard team developed its highly respected school of Human Resource Management. Lee Iacoca parleyed his hands-on management approach at Chrysler into a popular best seller. Philip Crosby made Quality Control an industry watchword. As management techniques they all have something to offer. They all work, but in different ways for different people at different times.

The ideas in this chapter are suggestions. It is just as important to try them on for size as it is that new suit. The way you manage your work needs to be as much an expression of your personality as the tie or blouse you wear to the office.

Management and Administration

When we speak of management, we mean the way people are personally supported and enabled to carry out their various tasks or roles. Management needs to be distinguished from administration. "Administration" can have the broad meaning of "a body of people exercising executive power," as when Americans refer to the Bush administration or the Clinton administration. Martin Saarinen uses "administration" in this way when he names good *administration* along with *energy, programs* and the ability to *include* newcomers as the four marks of a congregation in its prime.[2]

In this chapter, we will talk about administration in the much narrower sense as the aspect of management dealing with paper flow, information handling, communications systems, the provision of logistical services and backup.

Dorothy's desk was always covered with files, papers, books. There was no use putting material on her desk if you wanted her to see it. The church secretary and I figured out if you put something on her chair, she had to move it before she sat down. It proved to be an effective communication system.

My desk was just the opposite, cleaned off every night and the in-basket emptied every day. I handled each piece of paper only once. Projects were filed in folders. A do-list kept me on track. Surprisingly, both systems seemed equally effective. I kept print information moving through the office and into the hands of volunteers. Dorothy kept a lot of projects underway on her desk, but that often meant real thought went into them with fresh new ideas added as they came to mind.

My love of closure got projects off the desk and out working. Dorothy kept us from making decisions too quickly without enough consultation. We worked well together.

Keeping in Touch

There are four aspects to management: (1) ensuring that those charged with decision-making know the situation; (2) devising a plan, in collaboration with everyone involved, for carrying out decisions that are made; (3) coordinating the activity that puts the plan into action; and (4) keeping everyone informed about progress. If this sounds like communication, communication, communication — that is not far from the truth.

Management is quite a different thing from leadership. Leadership has been defined as "the process whereby one individual influences other group members toward the attainment of defined group or organizational goals."[3] Leadership includes working with a congregation to discern God's will, then providing the motivation that will free the congregation's energy and involvement. Management has to do with organizing the occasions when that planning can take place, maintaining the channels of communication along which the motivation can flow.

In their book, *In Search of Excellence*, Thomas Peters and Robert Waterman outlined eight characteristics of the well-run company. They are also characteristics of the well managed congregation. With some translation from business to church language, here are their management principles:[4]

1. **A bias for action**: Good management believes that "action removes the doubt that theory cannot solve." When in doubt, try it out. Whether it works or not will soon become apparent. Successful congregations do a lot of experimenting.
2. **Close to the community**: What are people coming to the church looking for? It may be meeting that need for friends, Sunday School for the children, dealing with a spiritual hunger, or just looking for a safe place to put one's life together after a crisis. Being in touch with people means you can discover what they really need, rather than what you think they need.

3. **Entrepreneurship**: Innovation is especially important for churches in these changing times. New trends in society require a creative response from the church.

4. **Getting it done through people**: The church succeeds that puts people first. Training people, motivating people, keeping in touch with people — that's the task of management.

5. **Hands-on, value driven**: Hands-on means the manager knows first-hand how the organization is working. Value driven management means delivering high quality with no compromising of integrity.

6. **Stick to the knitting**: Kennon Callahan and many others advocate a church grows by doing more of what it does best.[5] For an individual, stick to the management style you do best.

7. **Simple form, lean staff**: This is the KISS principle — keep it simple, saints. This does not diminish the importance of staffing for growth, but it does mean keeping staff assignments simple and focused on what is vital for growth.

8. **Simultaneous loose-tight administration**: That means loose control so that individual committees have lots of room to innovate and initiate, along with the tight communications that ensure you know what is happening and can offer support when it is needed.

Managing your Time

Time is the most precious commodity you have. And you only have it once. Here are some ways to use it rather than lose it.

Do a time study at least once every two years. Choose four weeks that are typical. Make a list of the categories you want to keep track of, either activities (leading worship, attending committee meetings, phoning, travelling, visiting, etc.) or programmes (Christian Education, Bible Study, Visitor Coordination, Sunday Worship, etc.) Make a chart with the work day divided into 15 minute blocks that you can carry on a clip board and keep track of what you do. In one study I realized I was spending six hours in the car each week, much of it delivering material. I started putting more notes in the mail and cut travel time in half.

Speed Leas, an American consultant who manages his time very well, has these suggestions I have found helpful:[6]

- Always phone for an appointment. Calling on people who are not there is not productive.
- Use a good date book, not just for appointments and meetings with others, but also to set aside time for projects and time off.
- Double up work and play. Golf with the Chair of the Board. My chairperson and I go jogging twice a week. It's a great opportunity to keep in touch.
- Keep three sets of files; active projects on your desk, files you refer to often in your desk drawer, information required less often in a filing cabinet.
- Forms save time. You need an expense form, visit report form, fax form, photocopy requisition form, marriage information form, baptism information form, worship service form. Create a form committees can use to indicate their plans for the year.

Speed Leas has an important caution. Most management books say to guard against interruptions. In a church where people come first, however, an interruption can be an opportunity for meaningful ministry. Time taken from ministry is not time saved.[7]

Energy is vital. You can often perform a task when energized in half the time. When you work through your do-list, alternate between activities that take energy and those that energize. If you're tired, take a break. Ten minutes smelling the roses can put spring in a whole day.

Computers

Computers can be the big time-saver, or a bigger time waster than you can imagine.

Most church applications require a word processing programme, a data base for address list, and financial management software. Make a list of everything you want your computer to do, then ask any reputable software dealer to tell you which programmes will do it best. Then ask what machine will best run that software. The key is your list of everything you need to do — get that right and the rest will follow.

It soaks up time to learn a new system. The few extra dollars it takes to buy an up-to-date machine and software means the system you buy will serve you years longer — and that means enormous amounts of time saved.

One person in each office should take the time to become computer literate by learning the jargon (bytes, RAM, etc.), keeping abreast of developments, knowing what equipment and software is the current industry standard. Don't rely on someone outside the office — they don't know all your processes unless they chart your information flow like a professional systems analyst. If your office expert knows how to do simple programming, that may be an asset. There are so many good professionally written software packages on the market, however, writing one's own is usually not cost efficient.

Computers are only tools to put the manager in touch with what is happening, which means in touch with people.

Zero Defects

Philip Crosby has pioneered the concept of zero defects. In industry this means making sure the automobile is built right as it is being put together. Depending on inspectors at the end of the assembly line to identify those that are defective is a good way to grow lemons.[8]

In the church, it means services and meetings that start and end on schedule, not just most of the time but all of the time. It means that readings in worship are done well, that sermons are meaningful, that the music is inspirational, that the service flows smoothly — every time.

It can't be done? It would cost too much in terms of time to ensure those high standards every time? What about the other costs, Philip Crosby asks, the cost of business that is lost, of replacing defective products? A church has to take into consideration the cost of losing that family who is church shopping and experiences your service on an off-week. They won't be back. Meetings that go on too long or wander have a cost — volunteers find excuses to drop out or do not agree to serve a second term. Rapid volunteer turn-over has enormous costs in terms of the time required for recruiting and training a constant stream of new people.

How do you maintain a "zero defects" church? Philip Crosby identifies four absolutes of quality control that we can apply to a congregation:

1. **What we mean by quality is having every aspect of the congregation's life conform to what the congregation has decided.** If the service is advertised as one hour, quality is measured by whether or not it takes one hour. If a volunteer is told there will be training, whether or not that training takes place and is done adequately is a measure of quality.

2.   **Quality is achieved through prevention.** Checking whether committees are missing things takes time. Pulling task forces together to patch up programmes takes more time. Better to develop a clear job description in the first place, so the committee or volunteer knows precisely what is expected.

3.   **The performance standard is zero defects.** Ninety percent satisfaction is not good enough. The illustration Crosby uses is whether you would be happy if only 10 percent of aeroplanes crashed. No crashes is the only acceptable standard. If we settle for less than the best, that is what will be delivered.

4.   **The measurement of quality is the price of non-conformance.** What does it really cost to have sloppy worship, poorly organized committee meetings, poor programmes? The real price needs to be measured in terms of lost members, lost commitment, lost opportunities for service, people lost to God's way and lost in life.[9]

This sounds like a lot to keep in mind, I know. But when good management practices are internalized and made part of you, they make management as an art possible. Once the techniques are mastered, they can be used in a way that embodies one's personality and communicates one's faith. Tall order, but it is true.

Good management is not all that visible, but it lays the foundation for every other aspect of a congregation's life. In their book *The Management of Ministry*, James Anderson and Ezra Earl Jones give an excellent description of the importance of leadership backed by management:

> In each generation and each place, the church seeks to re-
> define its reason for being, reexamine its fundamental task,
> understand the culture and concerns of its constituency,
> and work out methods for accomplishing its task. When it
> fails, the church becomes weak and disintegrates, and soci-
> ety weakens with it. When it succeeds, people's lives and
> entire societies are enriched.[10]

1   Michael Beer, et al, *Managing Human Assets* (New York: Macmillan, 1984).

2   Martin F. Saarinen, *The Life Cycle of a Congregation* (Washington: The Alban Institute, 1986).

3   Robert A. Baron and Jerald Greenberg, *Behavior in Organizations* (Boston: Allyn and Bacon, third edition, 1990), p. 374.

4   Thomas J. Peters and Robert H. Waterman Jr., *In Search of Excellence* (New York: Harper & Row, 1982).

5   Kennon L. Callahan, *Twelve Keys to an Effective Church* (San Francisco: Harper & Row, 1983), p. xvi. "The key decisions in long-range planning are the decisions to (1) claim, (2) expand, and (3) add to the congregation's strengths."

6   Speed B. Leas, *Time Management: A Working Guide for Church Leaders* (Nashville: Abingdon, 1978).

7   Leas, p. 111.

8   Philip B. Crosby, *Quality Without Tears: The Art of Hassle-free Management* (New York: Penguin, 1984).

9   *Ibid.*

10   James D. Anderson and Ezra Earl Jones, *The Management of Ministry* (New York: Harper & Row, 1978), p. vii.

Chapter 9

The Art of Managing Conflict[1]

According to Deuteronomy 14:7 and Leviticus 11:6, rabbits are
ruminants, i.e. the hare cheweth the cud! In the 19th century,
when conflicts between literalists and non-literalists were popular
someone wrote these lines of doggerel:
The bishops all have sworn to shed their blood
To prove 'tis true the hare doth chew the cud.
O bishops, doctores and divines, beware —
Weak is the faith that hangs upon a hare.[2]

It was First Church's organist that made the proposal. Glenn Gould's piano was for sale, the one he used to record the Goldberg Variations. A $40,000 grand piano for only $27,000. The choir saw the potential. Concerts in the church sanctuary. New vitality to the congregation's singing. The minister saw the potential. It would give the church organist, one of the finest in the city, a real reason to continue with the congregation. The Finance Committee saw only the price tag. "We can hardly meet all our expenses now. How are we going to raise $27,000?" The debate was heavy. Everyone had an opinion. The Finance Committee remained adamant. The Choir remained convinced.

A congregational meeting was called to decide and the vote resulted in a 55% majority in favour of buying the piano. The chair of the Finance Committee stood up. We weren't sure what to expect. "We've had our say," he said. "We've heard both sides. I'm still not convinced, but we've made our decision. Let's get the piano and get on with it."

On a scale of one to five, that conflict's a *one*. There's a difference of opinion, a hard decision to be made, a lot of unconvinced people, but in the end people trust the decision-making process and each other. This type of conflict can be handled by making sure the pro's and con's are all out in the open, that everyone's right to speak is honoured, that the decision-making process is fair, and that how people vote is not going to affect friendships or their place in the congregation. Eighteen months later, concerts sponsored by the choir together with donations had raised the whole $27,000. A happy ending.

The patriarch of Second Church's founding family came to the microphone during the announcement period. "This fracturing of hymns has got to stop!" They had been experimenting with changing the words of hymns to make them inclusive. A few weeks later the chair of the Worship Committee resigned. They were not adopting inclusive language fast enough. The choir had a running squabble with the choir director over his choice of anthems. Some would not sing anything that referred to God as "he."

This conflict was a *two* on the scale. Deeply held principles were involved. This was not a question of what was practical; this was a decision between right and wrong. Second Church worked six months to develop a policy. Compromise was the word. They agreed to disagree. They stopped making changes that offended the traditionalists. On the other hand, they didn't sing any hymns that were not inclusive either. A few people, like the choir leader, left for other congregations, but most felt the compromise was one they could live with. Five years later it was still a compromise, but it was working.

Another day, another situation. The parade of people into my office was continuous. Did I know how strongly people felt about the proposed merger of the two congregations that formed our pastoral charge? Did I know how caught off-guard they felt? The chair of the board, backed by a couple of friends, had been engaged in a mostly underground process to gather support for an amalgamation. They were using a vaguely worded resolution passed by the board to push for immediate action. Opposition was not long in appearing. Phone calls flew. Friends were called to secret meetings. Clusters whispered in the hall at coffee time. The needle was registering level *three* on the conflict severity scale.

A conflict type *three* requires fast action to prevent escalation. Get the meetings out in the open. Publicize the process by which a decision will be made, and set a time limit for the decision. Track down rumours and get the facts straight. Assure the parade to the office that action is being taken, and describe precisely what that is. Talk to individuals on both sides to keep communication as open as possible.

The board held an emergency meeting to rescind its earlier motion. A congregational meeting voted the merger down. The board chair and two other families left the congregation over the issue, but that was the end of it. The irony is that just a few years later, the congregations did decide to amalgamate. It wasn't so much the concept as the pushing and the pace that was the problem.

If the conflict is allowed time to fester, it escalates into a number *four*. People now start writing letters instead of just phoning. Positions are made public, and egos are put on the line. Everyone is pressured to take sides, and neutral ground disappears. In this atmosphere where everyone is under suspicion, including clergy, an outside consultant is mandatory. Reason can still prevail, but it takes time and skill to lower tempers and temperatures. Afterwards, healing takes time too.

Heaven save you from a level *five*. Half the Board at Fifth Church were adamant that the minister had to go. His message was "not of God!" They did not say where it was from, but their scowls left little doubt. "The problem had been going on for two years," they told the denomination's delegation sent in to bring peace. The dissident group had been underlining passages in the denomination's polity manual in red, passages that described their rights or indicated they were in the right. There had to be a congregational vote, the delegation decided. Voters lists were minutely examined. Names were challenged. Every step in the process was questioned.

In this type of conflict, lines have been drawn in the sand and a gulf separates the two sides. Communications have virtually ceased. The object now is to eliminate the opposition, fire the clergy, cleanse the congregation. The best a consultant can hope for is usually an amicable divorce. That is sometimes best for all parties. Within two years, the breakaway group from Fifth Church had fostered a thriving congregation of their own whose theology was much more to their liking. In the meantime, the clergy who had survived the vote of non-confidence reported the happiest years of his ministry within a unified congregation that supported and appreciated his approach.

Managing the Misconception

There is a misconception in the church that Christians just naturally all get along. If we don't, it is a sign we are not really Christians, something to be ashamed of. The fact is each of us is a unique human being, which means we are all different. Where there are differences, there are bound to be disagreements, tensions, and sometimes conflicts. To pretend there are no differences, in order to appear to get along effectively, kills honest communication, and eventually kills the congregation.

What we know is that a certain amount of conflict is actually beneficial. It releases energy, keeps a group open to new ideas, prevents the deep ruts that form from doing things the same way year after year.

In a parish that is an effectively functioning community people talk to one another until they understand why they have differences. When they can't understand, they still honour one another's good intentions.

The enemy of community is fear — fear of being different, fear of really revealing what we feel, fear of losing friendships, fear of conflict. The irony is that the more the Christian community values its community, the more susceptible it is to this kind of fear. When we have great community, people supporting and caring for one another, that is something we want to preserve. We are willing to put up with small irritants, sweep a few problems under the rug, because we are willing to make sacrifices for the friends and fellowship we have come to prize. That is all right if the differences are small. When major issues emerge, however, avoidance can be costly.

If my boss and I differ in a work situation, it is not generally a problem as long as my job is basically secure. If speaking out means I might be fired or eased out, then honesty can quickly cease to become the best policy. Fear enters the picture. The movie mogul, Samuel Goldwyn, is reported to have said, "I don't want any yes-men around me. I want people who will tell me the truth even if it costs them their job." That is not an environment where communications are likely to flow freely.

The worst case scenario results in what business consultant William Dyer calls "the Abilene paradox." Bill and his wife were visiting her parents in Coleman, Texas, on a stinging hot summer afternoon. They decided to drive 110 miles into Abilene in a car that was not air-conditioned to have what turned out to be a nondescript meal at a cafeteria. Only later did they discover not one of them wanted to go, but each was afraid to say so because they thought the others liked the idea and didn't want to be the one to spoil the fun. That kind of miscommunication happens a lot in churches, especially in congregations that specialize in being "nice."[3] We do well to remember that being "nice" is not always the best policy; honesty *is* better.

Jesus' Principles

Jesus taught three principles that are very helpful when it comes to keeping communications open for creative problem solving.

Integrity

"Let your yes be yes and your no be no," Jesus advised his followers (Mt 5:37). The way my parents put it was "Say what you mean and mean what you say." Today it is a question of whether we "walk the talk."

Integrity means following through on what we say we are going to do. Of course that means having thought out the implications before we make a commitment.

Integrity means our internal and external story are one and the same. The alternative is to do a lot of lying. The problem with lying is you have to remember what it is you told to whom. Being the same inside and out means you have only one story to remember, your own. Much simpler.

Paul reminded the Galatians "It is to freedom you are called." (Gal 5:13) The freedom to truly be who we are in every situation is one of the many gifts Christianity offers us.

Direction

In the Sermon on the Mount, Jesus told his followers not to be concerned about money or about food or clothing. These are distractions. "Set your mind on God's justice and God's new community, and all these other things will be yours as well," he told them (Mt 6:33).

Life needs to have direction, a single goal. When you know where you are going, you have at least a chance of getting there, even though life may throw in a detour or two along the way.

We read in another place that Jesus "set his face to go to Jerusalem." He knew where he was going, and that gave him an inner peace in the middle of what was to be the most difficult time of his life.

Identity

Jesus struggled with the question of his own identity. He spent time in the desert just after he had been baptized wondering about his mission and rejecting three inappropriate approaches. Midway through his ministry he asked his followers, "Who do they say I am?" "Who do you say I am?" The answer that had come at his baptism came again on the Mount of Transfiguration: "You are my beloved, my chosen." Churches must also struggle with the question of identity and may come up with different answers.

Identity is deeper than either integrity or direction. When the sense of identity is weak, one is very vulnerable to challenge, and to the anger that arises when a threat is real. When one's identity is so solid it cannot be threatened, there is an inner peace, and there is a sense of direction.

Jesus directed his thoughts about integrity, direction and identity to individuals. Christians have discovered these three characteristics are equally important for a congregation.[4]

Ways to Handle Conflict

There are many examples of conflict in the Bible. That should be our first clue to expect conflict in the Christian church. The good news is that the Bible also describes some very good ways to manage conflict. Take careful note of the context, however. Choosing the right approach for a particular situation is an art we have to work at and develop.

Confront

David had taken Bathsheba as his wife after doing away with her husband Uriah. Quite a wicked thing, but he was the king. The prophet Nathan appeared one day in David's court, supposedly to plead a case of injustice. It seemed a rich man, who had all kinds of sheep, had taken the one lamb possessed by a poor neighbour in order to feed guests. "This man who did this deserves to die," David pronounced in anger. "You are the man," replied Nathan. (2 Sam 12:1-9)

Leave

Jesus had reached the midpoint of his ministry. Crowds were coming. There was a lot of work to be done. He tried a new approach and sent his followers out in pairs to preach and heal, to do what he had been doing. One particular instruction was very insightful. "If people do not welcome you, leave that town and shake the dust from your feet." (Lk 9:1-6) When you are travelling life's highway, sometimes the best thing is to avoid on-coming traffic rather than get run over and put out of commission. As Christians we have to be conscious we have only so much energy. It is important to spend it in situations that will give the best return. Jesus did say to count the cost, didn't he?

Balance

"To whom should we pay taxes," they asked Jesus. It was a trick question. If he said to "Rome," he would offend the people's Hebrew nationalism. If he said "the temple," he risked denunciation to the occupying Romans as a trouble-maker. What he did say indicated some times it is best to bow to the realities of the situation, but keep your priorities straight in the process. "Render to Caesar what is Caesar's, and to God what is God's." (Lk 20:19-26)

Arbitrate

There were some early Christians who felt it was important to maintain all the Jewish traditions. Paul and others working with Gentiles found they had a particular problem with circumcision. The solution was to invite both sides to present their case at a special council called in Jerusalem. We are told that the discussion went on for a long time. It was James, believed to be Jesus' brother, who assumed the role of arbitrator. His ruling set out minimum requirements for new Christians, requirements that did not include circumcision. Sometimes, even in Christian circles, points of view are so deeply held that arbitration is the only way. Inclusive language and homosexuality are two areas where most denominations are experiencing irreconcilable differences. James had the respect of all sides, and his ruling was accepted. (Acts 15:1-21)

Second mile

The occupying Romans had a law allowing soldiers to conscript any civilian to carry their pack for them one mile. It was a hated symbol of bondage. Jesus had his prescription. "If anyone orders you to go one mile, go two miles with him." (Mt 5:41) Sometimes the best course of action is to just accommodate the other side. Do it their way, but do an even better job than they expect. No harm done, and you might just win a friend or two.

First Aid Until Help Arrives

In an accident where someone is injured, it is important for the first person on the scene to act quickly. Stop the bleeding, or at least keep the patient from moving and causing further injury. First aid can keep a critical situation from being life threatening. Fast action is just as important when a conflict situation begins to develop. Here are some first aid hints:

- Provide opportunities for people to speak and "get it off their chests."
- Do everything you can to increase the frequency, accuracy and comprehensiveness of communications.
- Reaffirm the values that people hold in common.
- Check out rumours. Words do get garbled in transmission.
- Identify the worst that could happen if the conflict is confronted squarely.
- Ensure that the decision-making process is clearly understood by everyone. People are usually willing to play by the rules, if they know what they are and if they are fair.
- Share examples of congregations who have dealt with similar issues successfully.

There is nothing like the light of day to put small issues in perspective, and provide a clear picture of the scope of major problems. When things are out in the open, they can be dealt with. It is important, though, that meetings are structured to encourage rational problem solving (adult approach) rather than defensive (child) or aggressive (parent) behaviours.

One last piece of advice, the one given by every patent medicine advertisement. If symptoms persist, see your doctor. The doctor, in this case, is an outside consultant with experience in collaborative problem solving. It may cost a little, but consider the cost if the conflict escalates out of control.

1   One of the best resource books in the church conflict area is: Speed B. Leas, *Moving Your Church Through Conflict* (Washington: The Alban Institute, 1985). Speed Leas is North America's foremost expert on conflict resolution. This material, which comes in a three ring binder, is very practical, very accessible.

2   Wayne Hilliker, "The Nature of Biblical Authority," *Gathering* (Summer/ Autumn, 1988).

3   William Dyer, *Team Building: Issues and Alternatives* (Reading, Mass: Addison-Wesley Publishing Company, 1977), p. 93.

4   Speed B. Leas and Roy Oswald, for example, noticed that a strong sense of identity was a common factor among congregations that were thriving. Roy Oswald and Speed Leas, *The Inviting Church* (Washington: The Alban Institute, 1987), p. 16f.

Chapter 10

The Art of Encouragement

The spirit of Don Quixote lives on in many Protestant leaders.
They dream of revitalized congregations and denominations,
even if it appears to be an impossible dream.

— William Easum, *Dancing with Dinosaurs.*[1]

The church is the place where we exercise the leadership of seeing things as they really are, and where we share our hopes and dreams. It is a community specially designed to be realistic about the present, and to dream a future that is the best of all possible worlds. What an amazing place!

We do have a few problems in creating a reality that matches our vision. There are, however, only five things to fix. When Willow Creek Community Church was being launched just north of Chicago, they did a survey to find why people did not attend church. The five reasons people gave were:[2]

- Church is irrelevant to my life. They use words I don't understand.
- It is boring. Everything is a dull, predictable routine.
- I always leave feeling depressed or guilty.
- They invade my privacy and embarrass me. They want me to stand up or sign a book or wear a tag.
- All they want is my money. They don't care about me.

The way to fix that would seem very easy:

- Use words that can be understood, even by someone not familiar with theological language. Then take the time to show how the insights of the Bible apply to everyday life.

111

- Build a surprise into every service of worship, every event. Keep it lively and interesting.
- Use every occasion to celebrate life, to build people up, to make people know they are loved.
- Honour people. Have tags and things to sign for extroverts, but do that in a way that allows introverts to have their privacy.
- Most important of all, care for each person for their own sake.

Communicate

In order to encourage people, it is certainly important to be in touch with where they are. The art of communication begins with listening. My wife writes novels for children aged ten to twelve. I notice every time she gets near anyone that age she is listening to the way they talk, watching the way they walk and communicate with each other. That way her books can reflect the vocabulary young people actually use and the characters will be true to life. In other words, they will communicate.

The art of communication in the church begins with listening to people — their questions, their problems, their hopes, their enthusiasms. There is not a lot of talk at a deep level in most of the casual conversations that take place over coffee or around a meeting. It is important to build intentional time into meetings to hear people and to really listen to people in casual conversations to hear what they are saying behind the words. We can ask "How are you?" in a casual way that invites a surface answer. Or we can ask "How *are* you?" in a caring way that invites deep sharing. It is then that listening begins to become ministry.

Ministry develops as we respond to what we have heard. I have only one rule — dig deep inside and become aware of what I am feeling and thinking, and share that openly and honestly. If I don't know what to make of it, that's what I say. If it isn't fair, I say so. If I can see some thread of purpose running through what has happened, I share that. It is this integrity, however, that encourages people, that says it is all right to be truly human.

To communicate means to polish. They tell me that every article in Time magazine is reviewed by 26 editors before it is published. The aim is to ensure the article is written in a way that truly communicates. In life, we polish our ability to communicate by inviting comments from friends, checking with colleagues before we act, making sure we are truly prepared and then prepared to change mid-stream if that is required to truly be in touch with others.

Surprise

I visited Orleans United Church just outside Ottawa the week before Easter. They were constructing a full size *papier maché* model of an empty tomb. The minister told me they try to have something new in the chancel every week, a surprise that welcomes people to worship and encourages them to come back the next week to find out what the new surprise will be.

Midlands United Church in Calgary has a six by eighteen foot blue cloth stretched across the front of the sanctuary. It is used to mount life size cloth figures that depict what is happening in the lectionary reading for that Sunday. One person has chosen as her ministry to prepare the figures and surprise people each week with a visual interpretation of the scripture. Kids love it, and adults feel cared for.

A certain amount of stability is important in the Sunday worship service. Most congregations follow a more or less standard order of service, sing mainly familiar hymns, strive for a fair degree of continuity in the pulpit. But there should be some excitement, some surprise, something new every week.

I happened to be visiting a congregation in St. Paul, Minnesota, on their anniversary. Everyone was given a red balloon. What a celebration. By the end of coffee time, all decorum had gone out the window and balloons were bounding everywhere.

In our daily ministry to one another, whether at work or in our home, surprise is a key ingredient. It takes a little thought, a little creativity, but it is incredibly encouraging.

People First

Pastor Wilson of Trinity Church of the Nazarene, California, has a philosophy I think Jesus would share: "If a congregation sets out to find hurts and heal them, it will never have to plead for money or search for new people. People and money will come to you."[3]

Seeing hurts and healing them is the essence of the gospel. Jesus' ministry consisted of discovering the particular need of the person and meeting that need. That means, of course, there are as many gospels as there are needs.

It does take money to run a church. I have encountered many congregations where people are tired from trying to balance the budget, spiritually squeezed from living too long in a financially pinched situation.

What we know is that the lack of money is just the symptom, not the problem. Think about the last time you were really involved in a project, one that excited you. You found the money for that, didn't you? I'm part of the team launching the Canadian Centre for Congregational Life. It is not easy. Some months we do not get paid very much. But we are helping people in small rural congregations, in inner city congregations missing their former glory, in suburban congregations who want to know how to best meet the spiritual needs of all those people around them. We are helping people help people. If you really care about people, the money will come — most of it from you — in order to do that caring.

Thank You

It is not possible to say "thank you" often enough to people. Those two words — thank you — are among the most encouraging in the English language.

I have gotten into the practice of launching each work day in the office of the small congregation I serve part time with a prayer that says "Thank you" to God for one of the members. It takes the form of a letter to that person, just a short note saying "thank you" for the contributions they have made and encouraging them to continue. The idea came from Steve Salee, pastor of a Methodist church in the United States. Don't write two letters, he said, that would be work. One is a meditation that is encouraging for me, and for the recipient.

The ways to say thank you are limited only by the imagination. Let yours fly free.

Courage

The hero of Paulo Coelho's book *The Alchemist* is a shepherd boy. The message is simple. "When I am truly searching for my treasure, I've discovered things along the way that I never would have seen had I not had the courage to try things that seemed impossible for a shepherd to achieve."[4]

To encourage means to give courage. We lived for two years in a small village in the mountains of Italy. When we arrived, the school was about to be closed, houses were deserted, the roads falling apart. We did a few things that did not last. What did happen, however, was our presence gave people from the village the courage to ask for the money for the roads, the courage to take their school seriously, the courage to fix up their houses. The telephone company put in a trunk line. The township paved the pathways. Encouragement proved infectious.

There are many people who have encouraged me through the years. The most encouragement, I find, comes when someone just walks along with me for a while. In simple language, we call it keeping each another company. True encouragement comes not so much from those who have pushed me into life, but from those who have journeyed with me and tackled life's challenges together with me. The ministry of walking beside someone is not to be neglected.

1   William Easum, *Dancing with Dinosaurs* (Nashville: Abingdon Press, 1993), p. 9.

2   Norman Shawchuck, et al, *Marketing for Congregations* (Nashville: Abingdon Press, 1992), p. 34.

3   Shawchuck, p. 99.

4   Paulo Coelho, *The Alchemist* (San Francisco: Harper, 1993), p. 137.

Chapter 11

The Art of Education

Education can either perpetuate the existing order and pattern of things or it can equip individuals with the necessary skills and knowledge to transform the world.

— Hank Zyp, *Change for Children* [1]

The committee wanted a way to illustrate that each child's contribution was important. It was Peace Sunday. "Little drops of water," someone on the committee said. "You know the song:

> *Little drops of water, in a mighty ocean*
> *We are sons and daughters of the one life."*

"It's not enough to just sing a song," said another of the committee members. "Not dramatic enough."

"What about having a container on one side of a balance arm," suggested someone. "When the container — we can mark it PEACE — gets full it will be heavier than the other end labeled WAR."

I volunteered to build the balance out of scrap lumber. It took two hours. War was symbolized by kitchen knives stuck into one end of the arm. An ice cream pail was fastened to the other end.

At story time, 15 children put cups of water into the PEACE pail to tip the scale and outweigh the knives of WAR. The point was made: individual contributions add up. The fact that the bucket hit the floor so hard that several knives fell out and water splashed us bystanders didn't hurt the drama of the situation one bit.

A Multiple Media Presentation

What do we mean by education? For me, education is a process of exploring how specific experiences relate to one another within an overarching system.

I feel heat coming from the stove. I observe a knob turned to "On." At some point I realize that these two experiences are connected. That is education at its simplest.

The more experiences the more there is to build on. That's why we try to make a child's life as rich as possible with bright colours around the crib, interesting things to look at, to touch, to put in the mouth. Then we help the child make connections between those experiences.

Education becomes an art when we are able to provide a child with enough experience to provide a rich environment, but not to the point where the experiences are so numerous and overwhelming that the child becomes confused and is no longer able to make connections.

Artists, be they painters, musicians, writers or actors, know a certain amount of poverty keeps the mind keen and primed for creativity. Too much poverty becomes debilitating and counter-productive. There is an art in maintaining that balance.

We human beings develop a rich repertoire of spiritual experience — experiences of awe, of joy, of gratitude. Sometimes we sense a loving spirit surrounding and accepting us, at other times a malevolent presence. Making sense of those experiences means seeing the relationship between them. Christians call the relationship between many of these "God." How many we attribute to God, and how many to malevolent spiritual forces or malignant aspects of the human personality depends on our theology.

A Check List

In order to have a rich educational program in a congregation, the first task is to ensure our bank of experience is full.

Do sermons and talks share stories that portray a variety of religious experiences? Stories encourage people to look for those experiences in their own life. Talking about the beauty of a sunset may encourage people to take a little extra time over the next sunset to ponder its beauty and the God behind that beauty.

Are participants personally involved? Addressing people by name is one way. It is also important that readings, stories or dramas physically and emotionally touch people.

Do church gatherings feature events that are in themselves experiences? When I was a boy coming home from church, my mother would ask "What did the minister say?" My boys ask, "What happened, Dad?" The event is what interests them.

Do the church sanctuary, Sunday School space and meeting rooms provide a rich visual experience? Words point to experience and depend on evoking memories in the listener or reader to give them power. A picture is an experience. My favourite church in all the world is Santa Susanna's in Rome. It is light and bright, with walls a riot of biblical images. What I appreciate is not the story told by the pictures so much as the artistic energy that radiates out of the walls and permeates my being. Attending mass there is truly an experience.

Learning Styles

A few months, ago my co-worker Joyce Madsen came into the office out of breath, face flushed with excitement. She had just discovered she was a kinesthetic learner. All her life she had thought less of herself because images didn't stick in her memory like they seemed to for others. She enjoyed listening, but the words did not stay with her. Maybe there was something wrong with her.

She had just participated in a seminar and discovered that there are three ways of learning, not just two. In addition to those whose primary learning style is visual or auditory, many people are kinesthetic. Joyce can tell you the emotion of participants at a meeting a year ago, the feeling she experienced in a certain place. She can describe in detail the ambiance of a church sanctuary. Just don't ask her what the place looked like.

My primary learning mode is visual. I can see the page that holds the information I am trying to remember. I can visualize an automobile motor operating in three dimensions.

In one particular workshop we always showed the movie, "Requiem for a Heavyweight." One night the sound bulb burnt out half-way through and there was no replacement. Two of my colleagues remembered the dialogue so well that they just dubbed it in as the silent movie went along. I was impressed. They were auditory learners.

You can tell which of the three learning styles a person favours by listening to the figures of speech they prefer. Visual learners say things like:
I see the light.
Let's focus on that.
I see what you mean.
Can you picture that?

Auditory people prefer sounds:
That's clear as a bell.
Can we talk?
Keep your ear to the ground.
That rings true for me.

Wolfgang Amadeus Mozart was certainly an auditory learner. Having heard a piece of music, he could walk to the piano and play it through flawlessly from beginning to end. When composing, the music grew in his mind.

> ... my subject enlarges itself and ... though it be long,
> stands almost complete and finished in my mind. ... Nor do
> I hear in my imagination the parts successively, but I hear
> them, as it were, all at once. What a delight this is, I cannot
> tell. ... What has been thus produced, I do not easily forget.[2]

Kinesthetic or feeling people can dazzle you with their innate ability to sense the ambiance of a room and remember emotions long after a gathering. Theirs is a world of joy, love, hurt, happiness, sadness and gladness. They say "I have a gut feeling," or "I sense you are right."

It is important in an educational process to provide a variety of learning approaches or techniques that appeal to all three styles — visual, auditory and kinesthetic. It helps to know which learning style each participant prefers.

In a worship service we use music, which is primarily auditory. We use liturgy, which is again auditory. And we have a sermon, again auditory. For visual impact we often depend on a few stylized saints peering down from stained glass windows. Many congregations today use banners that are truly works of art, rich in colour and symbolism.

We pay attention to acoustics and visual impact. It is just as important to design in the feeling you want to communicate. It is an exercise in kinesthetic awareness to walk into a sanctuary and ask "What does this room say to me emotionally?" "What are the feelings that it evokes in me?" If the answer is coldness or loneliness, work is needed. A feeling of friendliness and warmth can be enhanced through warm colours, the use of wood, open design and textured fabrics.

Mentors

My son Peter learns best by doing. Walk him through the process of tuning a car motor, and he has it for life. He makes the best pasta salad you have every tasted, having learned how in a "hands-on" cooking class.

When I was living in Rome learning Italian, the language records worked well in the beginning. Then I found I needed someone alive to talk to, someone who would push me where I needed pushing, someone to really have a conversation with.

A mentor is someone a little farther along on the journey who can guide you. You relate best to a mentor who is a half generation older — ten years say — someone more like an older sibling than a parent. A mentor doesn't just describe the road ahead, he or she walks you along it. You learn as much by living and watching as by what they say.

When I was fifteen, I had Scout leader who was a mentor. He was twenty-five or so. He showed us how to work together in our patrols by working with us. My first job was bagging potatoes in his grocery store. Our troop took our bikes apart and put them together again in his basement. We went to his wedding and saw him set up married life.

There is a dynamic to mentoring. The best description I know of is in Daniel Levinson's book *The Seasons of a Man's Life*.[3] In the beginning, a mentoring relationship is much like a love affair. A mentor is someone whose values, lifestyle, and approach you want to emulate, someone you intuitively trust, so all the barriers to learning come down and you soak up everything he or she says and does. It is an immersion style of learning. In the next stage, you work with the mentor more as a partner. You bring more and more to the relationship, and mutual learning takes place.

There may come a point when you begin to see your mentor's flaws, ways you could do it better. Perhaps your mentor resists your suggestions. Communication and sharing decrease, ideas of how to do things diverge. The separation can be as stormy as a contested divorce, or it can be more a graduation amid feelings of mutual appreciation as you move on to new areas of endeavour.

Developing mentoring as an art means being clear about the dynamics. It is the artist that can develop a mentoring relationship to the point where spiritual skills and Christian values are shared, then let the relationship evolve into a friendship of equals that provides a lifetime of mutual support.

Many educational programs assign a mentor to graduates to help them make the transition from the classroom to the real world. The church, with its multi-generational membership, is an ideal place to develop mentoring relationships. Whether it is through the men's club, women's circle, youth group or confirmation class — all can facilitate the formation and development of mentoring partnerships.

Bringing Children on Board[4]

During ages one to three, children develop a sense of autonomy — discovering themselves as separate from others. We honor this age group by treating them as individuals. Each of them gets their own balloon, their own toy. We encourage them to participate in church functions on their own terms. When this happens they receive the message that God accepts each of us as the unique individuals we are.

At ages four and five, children begin to develop a sense of initiative, putting forward their own thoughts and ideas. It is crucial, at this stage, to accept and celebrate their first offerings, incorporate their ideas into stories. They love participating in songs with actions or they can contribute words. One I wrote to the tune "Alli Balli Bee" goes like this:

> Plant the *seed* in the ground
> God makes the sun go round and round.
> God makes the rain to fall.
> God makes the *grass* grow big and tall.

The children get to choose what they want to plant in each verse, a *kernel* becomes *corn*, an *acorn* becomes an *oak*, a *bulb* becomes a *tulip*.

From six to eleven, children become industrious, exploring the world around them and experimenting with how it works. They were doing this when they put the water in the bucket and contributed to peace winning over war. Children this age are attracted to magic, and a bit of conjuring can be used to suggest that wonders lie beneath the surface of life.

One morning we invited our children to share the message "God Loves You" with the congregation. We produced a box of paper airplanes, each inscribed with these words. The messages not only went out, they were eagerly caught by normally stern adults who threw them on to others, smiles lighting their faces. There was a sense of excitement in the air. No amount of talk could have communicated as powerfully the emotion of acceptance in the room.

Children only begin to understand abstract concepts like "hope" and "salvation" at ages 12 to 15. To develop this understanding, they need to be able to relate these concepts to concrete experiences, as mentioned at the start of this chapter. It is important, then, to be familiar with the type of experiences that enliven the life of a person beginning their teens.

Theological Worlds

At one time, the Christian church assumed the problem every person had was guilt. The solution was to assure them of God's forgiveness, if they would just confess their sins — in effect acknowledge they had something that needed forgiving.

Then something strange began to happen. Person after person said they did not feel particularly guilty. Evangelists were accused of trying to make people feel guilty whether they were or not so they could be forgiven. Theologians wondered out loud whether God was not more loving than we had previously been led to believe. Encouraged by Matthew Fox, most mainline churches are in the process of discarding or downplaying the concept of original sin championed by Augustine in favour of a doctrine of original blessing that sees humans beings as essentially good. More and more people want the freedom to reach their potential, not follow a multitude of restrictive rules and regulations.

Some very creative work has been done by the American theologian W. Paul Jones. His book *Theological Worlds* develops a scheme that lets us see the traditional Christian perspective as one element in a larger picture. He argues there is not just the one problem of guilt that encourages theological reflection, but five key problems for which there are five religious answers — five "theological worlds" if you will.[5]

For the inhabitants of Theological World 1, the problem is *separation* and the answer is *reunion*. These people feel abandoned, separated from God, separated from the ground of being. The answer is to find a spiritual home, to experience reunion of their spirits with the Spirit of God.

The theologian Paul Tillich talks about this as the moment when our isolation and loneliness are overcome in a profound experience of acceptance. "Sometimes at that moment, a wave of light breaks into our darkness, and it is as though a voice were saying: 'You are accepted. YOU ARE ACCEPTED.'"[6]

The problem for World 2 people is *conflict*, and the answer is *vindication*. They see conflict at the heart of life and of nature. Life is a drama with winners and losers. Death is the final enemy. Hope comes from the faith that God's will is going to eventually triumph. Our role is to commit ourselves to God's side in the struggle. Every victory is a foretaste of the final victory.

World 3 people struggle with a feeling of *emptiness*. They long for the sense of *fulfillment* that will fill the void at the centre of their being. They feel estranged from self, invisible, impotent, insignificant. The answer is to begin to realize one's potential, to discover a caring community where you are significant. The Christian realizes that "God loves me for who I am." If we are to love our neighbour as ourselves, we must first learn to love ourselves. That is the reality this approach honours.

Jones' World 4 is the traditional Christian *condemnation* and *forgiveness* model. "We have erred and strayed from thy ways like lost sheep," a traditional confession reminds us. "We have followed too much the devices and desires of our own hearts; we have offended against thy holy laws." The answer is to ask God's forgiveness. The paradox of the Christian life is that God forgives the unforgivable, loves the unlovable, and accepts the unacceptable.

World 5 is the area where *suffering* obscures all other ways of looking at reality, and *endurance* is the only response. This approach speaks to the poor who cannot escape their poverty, the incurably ill who have little hope of health, the marginalized who dare not defy their oppressors. We may not be able to escape suffering, but we have the choice of giving in to self-pity, or living to the full the life we have.

Each of these is a legitimate response. There are Christians for example, who support each one of the five perspectives. The same is true of the major faiths of the world, although each has traditionally stressed one or other of the responses:

- Hinduism hopes for eventual reunion with Brahman, the underlying reality (World 1: separation/reunion).
- The word "Islam" means submit. Mohammed assured his followers that if they would submit to Allah, the ultimate victory would be theirs (World 2: conflict/vindication).
- New Age Religion offers dozens of ways to fill the emptiness of life and achieve our potential (World 3: emptiness/fulfillment).
- Traditional Christianity, as we have said, stressed the World 4: condemnation/forgiveness model.
- Buddhism sees all life as suffering, with salvation coming through developing a detached compassion (World 5: suffering/endurance).

The art is to identify the perspective from which each person starts their religious journey. Only then can education give the guidance that will take them to their desired destination.

Education as an Art Form

When I was growing up there was a radio program called, "It pays to be ignorant." The moderator would ask a completely objective question, which usually contained the answer. "Who was buried in Grant's Tomb?" "In what year did the War of 1812 take place?" The panel would then proceed to reflect on that question. "Was it a white tomb?" "Where is it located?" "I really don't like tombs much. I'd rather talk about where Grant was born."

Then would come the interpretations. "Tombs are basically undemocratic, because the famous get bigger ones than anyone else." "So life is undemocratic. What's so special about death that it should be different?" Finally the panel would express the decision they had reached. "When I die, I don't want to be buried in a tomb."

They never got around to answering the original question. It was a rather silly show, but it was profoundly educational because education is a journey through precisely those four levels of understanding:

- **Objective:** Just the facts, nothing but the facts.
- **Reflective:** My reactions to the facts. Reflecting on relationships between facts.
- **Interpretive:** What I understand this is all about.

- **Decisional or Theological:** What I have decided to do about it —
  or — What God is calling me to do about it.

Each session, each class, each meeting, each prayer time can be a journey through these four levels of understanding.

Becoming educated is not an easy journey, but it is a profound journey, as anyone who has taken it will attest. It is a voyage of discovery that explores the meaning of life, and then allows what we discover to inform the life decisions we make.

1   Hank Zyp, *Change for Children* (October, 1987): 24.

2   Quoted in Michael Brooks, *Instant Rapport: The NLP Program that creates intimacy, persuasiveness, power!* (New York: Warner Books, 1989).

3   Daniel J. Levinson, *The Seasons of a Man's Life* (New York: Ballantine Books, 1978), pp. 97–101.

4   Information in this section is drawn from the article: Denise Davis-Taylor and Clair Woodbury, "Connecting kids with God," *pmc* (January 1988): 20 ff.

5   W. Paul Jones, *Theological Worlds* (Nashville: Abingdon, 1989).

6   Paul Tillich, *The New Being* (New York: Scribner's, 1955): Sermon, "You Are Accepted."

Chapter 12

The Art of Giving

Kindness in words creates confidence, kindness in thinking creates profoundness, kindness in giving creates love.

— Lao-Tzu

Our son David was ten years old when he began his first paper route. Delivery was to the homes of the other teachers at St. Andrew's boys school in Aurora just north of Toronto. He was young, but the houses were all on the school property and there weren't all that many. That Christmas, when I opened my presents, there was an "N" gauge train from David. A perfect miniature. I was overwhelmed. He had used the first money from his paper route to buy his father a train.

David is now 35 and we still have that train. It has a new locomotive, new track and new signals (but it is the same train). It is one of the most precious gifts I have ever received. What makes it precious? The *cost* for one thing; all the money my son had. Also the *enduring* quality — it has lasted all these years. The *usefulness* of it — we bring it out every Christmas and it ties our celebration into all the great Christmases our family has had in the past. Its power as a *symbol*, as a reminder of a son's love.

There is an art to ensuring the gifts we give embody all four of these qualities.

Life is God's Gift to Us

We have been given a fantastic gift by God. We have shown up. We did not ask to be alive, we are just here.

How should we celebrate that gift? By making our life a fantastic one, yes. But there is more. At Christmas or whenever we receive a gift, we celebrate that gift by:

- saying *thanks* to the person who has given the gift to us;
- trying it on or *using* it in some way;
- *continuing* the spirit of giving, giving a gift to someone else.

Celebrating the gift of life has the same dynamics for us. The way to celebrate that gift is by saying "thank you" to God. If we are not clear about the nature of God, what God is like, we can still say thank you to whatever brought us this incredible gift.

"Thank you" is a magic phrase when you think about it. It *acknowledges a debt*; that is, it indicates we know who the gift came from and that it is something of value. It also *pays the debt*. A thank you is all parents expect from their children — that, and the affection in their hug, pays the debt.

We can also celebrate by "trying life on." That means using it, experimenting with it, bringing the best out of it. This can mean risk, and many of us like to play it safe. Two caterpillars watched a butterfly. One said to the other, "You'll never get me up in one of those things!"

The Church today — more than ever before — needs people willing to risk. The church needs people who can dream and imagine new ways to minister to others and who are not afraid to put their dreams into action.

We also celebrate by continuing the spirit of giving. We pass it on. We have children, give our best to others, contribute to our neighbour and to all of civilization.

What gifts can we give? There are basically two, and they make giving an art. One gift has to do with thinking — being clear about the way life really is. The other gift has to do with feelings — being there with people, for people.

The Way Life Is

"The first responsibility of a leader is defining reality."[1] While it is clear that leaders draw their inspiration and spiritual reserves from their sense of stewardship, much of the leverage leaders can actually exert lies in helping people achieve more accurate, more insightful, and more empowering views of reality.[2]

Giving a clear view of reality! How seldom do we think of our contribution that way. Yet what is more valuable than the ability to see things as they really are?

"Now we see only puzzling reflections in a mirror," says J. B. Phillips' translation of 1 Corinthians 13. "When we meet God we shall see face to face." Those who meet God, whether in the privacy of their own prayer life, in the corporate worship experience, or in relating to the world of nature, expect — whether they can define it or not — a "clearer view of reality."

If Jesus did one thing, it was to help those who came to him to see life more clearly — as it really was. Churches often use a response after the gospel reading. The one I like best is: "Thanks be to God for this, the truth about life."

It is important to honour the fact that each one of us sees in a different way. I heard Dr. Robert McClure being interviewed over radio a number of years ago. When he was serving as a United Church of Canada medical missionary on the island of Taiwan, the interviewer asked, and he encountered Buddhists, how did he acknowledge their Buddhism while maintaining his Christian perspective? His answer is the key to honouring one another in this pluralistic world. "I have a pair of glasses that have been prescribed for my eyes. They fit me very well and allow me to see clearly. Your glasses are different, because they are designed to let you see clearly. I hope your religion lets you see life as clearly as my religion lets me."

It is also important to recognize the growing realization of the unity that underlies our diversity. Joseph Campbell, who did so much to give us an understanding of the role of myth in our lives, said: "When you see the earth from the moon, you ... realize again your close relationship with the animals and with the water and the sea. ... You don't see any divisions there of nations or states. This might be the symbol, really, for the new mythology to come."[3] That view from the moon gives us the view that we Christians have had all along. Now is the time to celebrate the gift that understanding is to humanity.

The Gift of Sharing

Seeing things as they really are has to do with clear thinking. The second gift is the gift of sharing — sharing our excitement about life, being there for others and with others. This relates to feelings.

In the movie *Mrs. Dellafield Wants to Marry* the bride played by an aging Katharine Hepburn and the equally elderly groom read: "Reach out and touch another hand and celebrate with us the joy of life on this astonishing earth." Their two families, one Jewish and the other Protestant, have been resisting the wedding, but reach out and take each other by the hand in a moving scene of recognition, acceptance and coming together.[4]

Sharing is particularly important where there is poverty, and the injustice that poverty brings with it. Henri Nouwen observed when he was in South America, "Poverty is so much more than lack of money, lack of food, or lack of decent living quarters. Poverty creates marginal people, people who are separated from that whole network of ideas, services, facilities, and opportunities that support human beings in times of crisis."[5] The challenge to us in North America is truly to be there for the third world, to share truly, not just a few dollars, but the kind of sharing the church is best at, people-to-people sharing.

Helping Each Other Share

Giving is an art that develops with practice. That means the church is not only a place where we share, but also a place where we learn to share. That is important to realize. People who associate with a church for the first time generally have a lot of growing to do when it comes to giving. It takes a process of growth to become middle givers, then mature givers.

Kennon Callahan's book on stewardship[6] says that occasional contributors and new households — *beginning givers* in my terminology — are motivated by compassion and by community.

By *compassion*, he means a real, obvious human need. The pastor makes an appeal during the service, "There is a refugee family that needs help financing the air ticket for their brother who is in danger in his home country." The money is pressed into his hand by a number of people at the end of the service.

By *community*, Callahan means that we support what makes it possible for us to meet and be together. Even people who have just walked through the door know the church needs funds to pay for heat and light, to do building repairs, to pay for staff to coordinate and lead gatherings. That's community.

Middle givers are practical people. They are motivated by *reasonability*. They give when it is reasonable, when it makes good sense to give. They have one eye on the budget and give enough to meet the bills. Just enough, not too much. The other eye is on the benefits. How cost effective is this operation?

Mature givers are motivated by commitment and challenge. They have a *commitment* to supporting the church as an institution. Giving is a symbol of faithfulness to God and to their Christian beliefs. They respond and give sacrificially to aspects of the church's life where they are personally committed. Mature givers also respond to a *challenge*. They want their contribution to make a difference.

A rabbi, a priest and a minister were great fishing buddies. One Monday, on their day off, they were out fishing in a stream that the rabbi had recommended. He got his line snagged on a rock, got out of the boat, walked across the water, freed the line, and walked back to the boat. Again it happened. Snag, walked across the water, freed the line, back into the boat. The priest snagged his line. Rabbi got out of the boat, walked across the water, and freed the line.

When the Protestant minister snagged his line, his mind was already working. If the rabbi could do it, why not he. He got out of the boat, and was going down for the third time, when his friends pulled him, wet and sputtering, into the boat.

"How did you do that?" he asked the rabbi. "How did you walk across the water."

"It's easy," replied the rabbi, "when you know where the stones are."

Helping people to grow in the art of giving is easy, when you know what motivates them, what the stepping stones are to mature giving.

Type of Motivation

Beginning Givers Like Information

In 1994, I was involved in a research project to identify the factors affecting financial support in new congregations. My research partner Yvonne Stewart and I interviewed 28 people from five United Church congregations: Mount Seymour in North Vancouver, Riverbend in Edmonton, Orleans just outside Ottawa, Eden in Mississauga and Knox in Lower Sackville, Nova Scotia.

We asked each congregation for an interview with two givers considered in the top category by the treasurer of their congregation, two in the middle and two at the lower end of the spectrum. When we analyzed responses, we discovered real differences in what people said motivated them to increase their financial support.

The low category givers were mostly new to the United Church. Only two out of ten had been active in the United Church before coming to their current congregation. Almost all the medium and high givers had solid United Church backgrounds. That might have considerable bearing on the importance lower givers place on good information about the actual needs of the congregation. They told us it helped to know about mortgage payments and the money needed to operate the facility. "There was a thermometer right at the door into the sanctuary that made us think."

Knowing what to give was reported by beginning givers as an important factor. "It was after reading something about giving a proportion of your salary that we felt it would be appropriate to increase our giving from $5 to $10 and sometimes $20." When income increases, there is a tendency to give more to the church.

Special appeals are important too, especially when they are for something practical but not too expensive. "We decided to open a food bank. We put out a call and within three weeks we had about $1,000. People are willing to give if it is something they can see as really important and essential to the life of the church."

What Motivates Givers to Increase Support for their Church

LEVEL OF GIVING

	Info. about financial needs	Increase in income	Knowing what to give	Special Appeals	Building, special program or physical projects	Involvement in church activities
Mature Givers		Increase in income		Special Appeals	Building, special program	Involvement in church activities
Middle Givers	Info. about financial needs				or physical projects	
Beginning Givers	Info. about financial needs	Increase in income	Knowing what to give	Special Appeals		

Middle Givers are Practical

Middle Givers also respond to information about the regular financial needs of the congregation. "We had been told our mortgage on the church was large. Not that they're asking us to give the money to pay off the mortgage, but it was a factor. We know it is a big mortgage."

Middle givers also mentioned the importance of digging deeper for larger projects like a building program or major physical projects. "When they built the church, that's when our givings really jumped."

Mature Givers are Involved

Those in the higher giving category tended to be much more involved with the church, and that involvement resulted in a higher financial commitment. Three high givers had served as envelope secretary for their congregation. All reported their giving took a major jump when they saw what others in the congregation were contributing.

Others were involved on the Board, and that gave them insight into the real needs of the congregation. "About six months after we got here and my wife joined the Finance Committee, we became aware of the financial situation of this particular congregation. We sat down and discussed it in detail, thought we could probably do more, so at that point we doubled our givings."

Some were involved in a specific program, and made a special contribution to ensure the program had the equipment and funds required to do an effective job. There was a tendency to take ownership of projects and respond personally to special appeals. High givers reported having a hand in furnishing a chapel, finishing a classroom, contributing chancel furniture.

High givers were open to sharing increased income they felt was a gift to them. "Life has been good and I can afford to give more."

Some 2,500 years ago the Chinese philosopher Lao-Tzu wrote, "Kindness in words creates confidence, kindness in thinking creates profoundness, kindness in giving creates love."[7] That was the thought that opened this chapter. What we learn in the church is the art of giving in a way that it creates love — a noble art indeed.

1   Max De Pree, *Leadership is an Art* (New York: Dell Publishing, 1989), p. 11.

2   Peter M. Senge, *The Fifth Discipline: The Learning Organization* (New York: Doubleday, 1990), p. 353.

3   Joseph Campbell, *The Power of Myth* (New York: Doubleday, 1988), p. 33.

4   Movie: *Mrs. Dellafield Wants to Marry*. (Made for TV movie, 1986).

5   Henri J. M. Nouwen, *Gracias! A Latin American Journal* (New York: Harper & Row, 1983), p. 117.

6   Kennon Callahan, *Giving and Stewardship* (San Francisco: Harper, 1992).

7   Lao-Tzu, founder of Taoism, c. 604-531 B.C.

Chapter 13

The Art of Social Action

Action removes the doubt that theory cannot solve.

— Author unknown

*T*his quotation was one of Joe Matthews' favourites. He was the founder of the Ecumenical Institute of Chicago. With nine others, he and his wife moved to Chicago from Texas, purchased a former seminary in the heart of the black west-side ghetto, and set about to renew the neighbourhood and the church. In the 60's, some 15,000 people a year signed up for their weekend "Religious Studies One" course. By 1975, 1,500 volunteers were serving in 100 social action projects in 17 nations, all patterned on what that first crew had learned in their Chicago pilot project.

They were obviously doing something right. For me it was the way they listened, their courage in tackling the hardest problem first, and the creativity that constantly tested possible ways of dealing with the situation. Underneath was a profound respect for Jesus' way of doing things.

Ears to Listen

A Calgary congregation was interested in being more in touch with the people in their neighbourhood. The census data said there were some wealthy areas in the community and also some areas where family incomes were much lower than average. They visited all the local social agencies, churches and schools to ask for their advice. "You know the problems for people who live in this area. Which ones could our congregation help with?" The opportunity that best matched the gifts of people in the congregation was a school serving one of the low income areas. People were needed to read to children in class, to provide lunches, to collect and sort books for the library, to support the teachers. Real bonds have been established that have given the congregation energy, expanded friendships across community lines and created a project that truly reaches out into the community. It all began with listening for the real needs.

I was part of the team that launched a village development project high in the mountains of central Italy. Termine di Cagnano is a small community of 200 people at the end of a mountain road, a village that development had passed by. The fact that they all voted Christian Democrat in a township with a Socialist-Communist council did nothing to help their cause.

An initial consultation created a long list of the more obvious problems. There were only three telephones in the whole community. The school was scheduled to close at the end of the year. Young families were moving away. Abandoned houses lined every street in town. The list went on and on.

We made a start on some of the local problems. A village family donated one of their unused houses as a social centre. We found the money to hire a couple of young village women to start a pre-school in the local Catholic church. We painted the school rooms. We hired a young man to help make traditional beech-wood bread chests in the local carpenter shop.

We began to find ears who would listen — in the government bureaucracy in Rome, in the provincial agriculture department, at the township Mayor's office. They were listening, but not much was happening.

Then our listening began to pay off. We heard from several sources about the feud between the township and the Catholic church. The church had started a pre-school that no longer existed. We knew about that, because we were using their facility for our pre-school. Trouble began when the township announced it was building a new secular pre-school on the edge of town. Its funding cut off, the church pre-school died. Left out of the process, the priest warned people not to go to the new school. There it sat, never used, windows smashed, roof tiles broken, floor flooded.

Go for the Central Problem

We walked around that abandoned building many times before we realized it symbolized all that was holding the village back — the division between the church and the township council, bad planning, local vandalism.

It took all our energy for 12 months to activate a cooperative to use the building, negotiate a lease from the township, repair the building itself, find a loan for machinery, train local people to operate a furniture factory, and locate a market for the product. We did nothing but work on the building for a year. When we looked up, we saw the roads were being paved by a township council who managed to locate money lost in the bureaucracy for years, houses were being renovated by families from Rome who had new hope for the village, farmers were working together because they had seen what a furniture cooperative could do.

On opening day, the priest and mayor stood side by side; the priest said the blessing and the mayor cut the ribbon. The priest took over as master of ceremonies and the mayor took over as master of rhetoric. We had only worked on a building, but the result had been the renewal of the spirit of the village.

Power to the People

There is an irony to the end of the story. We went back for a visit three years later. The furniture cooperative was no longer functioning. The products we had made were too complex, markets too distant. The village, however, was thriving. The phone company had put in a 50 line trunk. Village roads and pathways had been paved. The school was alive and well. By tackling the toughest problem, we had freed everyone else to solve the other problems.

There comes a point in every social action project where you are really proud of what you have done. It is only natural to want to hang on to some of the glory. Part of a painter's art is knowing when to declare the painting finished. A novelist needs to know when editing has done as much as it can. In the same way, there is a real art in knowing when to leave a project. The project may not be done, but your part in it may well be complete. The real purpose, after all, is not to repair buildings or open factories, but to give back to people control of their lives.

Some needs go on. The congregation I have been a member of has a project to help single mothers with nutrition and budgeting for their families. Children are cared for while a social service professional does the actual training.

I learned a lot by doing a social action project in another country. I was really dependent on the people there, particularly since I didn't speak the language all that well and was a guest in the country. That was good, because the project would not have worked if it had not empowered the local people. Here, in North America, the needs are all around us too. There is no shortage of opportunities to reach out a helping hand or to speak out for justice in a situation where people are being exploited. It is just the temptation to take charge is greater. Power to the people is not just a slogan, it is the way to truly be of service.

Creativity is Crucial

When you think about the changes that are needed in this world — and reading any daily paper will produce a very long list — it is obvious that creativity is very important. When resources are limited, it is a matter of acting smarter. Creativity lets the Christian do more with less — and do it better.

One way to spark creativity is to immerse yourself in the situation until both the situation itself and the possibilities for change become clear. The social activist brings certain skills and resources, but the greatest contribution is a vision of a better way. Knowing there is a better future, even if the way ahead seems hidden, opens the door for that creative urge to operate.

I find pushing myself to write something down stimulates creativity. It helps to clarify my thinking. I'm just enough of a story-teller that I want to know how the story ends. That releases the creativity as I imagine what the ending might be.

Joe Matthews used to keep creativity alive in the Ecumenical Institute of Chicago by renaming the departments regularly. It had the effect of breaking up old ways of thinking, marking a new beginning, releasing new energy. What's in a name? A great deal, I came to discover.

Another way to stimulate creativity is to push for three alternate scenarios for any given situation. My first idea is often what I want to happen and the second is what I think ought to happen. When I push for a third possibility I may just stumble on what God wants to happen.

The Jesus Way

Is there any doubt that Jesus was a social activist? He had to walk very carefully, of course. The occupying Roman Empire dealt very harshly with anyone who agitated for change. Careful as he was, his enemies managed to have him executed on the charge that he had declared himself a king.

He told a parable about workers who received the same pay, whether they had worked in the vineyard all day, started at noon, or had been hired an hour before quitting time. That was very subversive talk, even by today's standards.

Jesus was a master of asking the probing question that dropped debate from the legal to the spiritual level. He put humanitarian principles before religious practices. There was a subtlety to Jesus' advice. "If one of the occupation troops forces you to carry his pack one mile, carry it two miles." (Mt 6:41) That would make a soldier wonder, wouldn't it? Perhaps even shame him a little — or imply you were as free to decide to carry a pack as he was free to give orders.

Paul develops Jesus' concept of radical equality to its logical conclusion. "There is no difference between Jews and Gentiles, between slaves and free, between men and women; you are all one in union with Christ Jesus." (Gal 3:28) There are still pockets of resistance to that in the church today, two thousand years later.

Do's and Don'ts

Don't become a social action fanatic. It is not your place to become angry at others for not taking up your cause. God may have other work for them to do that is equally important.

Do probe until you get past expressed needs to real needs. It takes a lot of building of trust until people really open up and share those places where their need is greatest, because that is also where they are most vulnerable.

Don't look for the easy answer. Don't give fish, teach how to fish. Don't give a house, share how to build a home. That way people not only develop a sense of ownership, they also become colleagues.

Do stop and listen for a long time *before* you act. Once committed it is hard to turn back. The way the United States carried on the Vietnam War a decade after large numbers of people saw its absolute futility demonstrated that for me.

Do what you are good at, and ask others to do what they are good at. Jesus was good at healing. Crowds came to be healed, and stayed to listen. Some people are great at collecting signatures on a petition. Others can organize a trip to Guatemala. Social action is a lot of people doing a lot of different things.

Do experiment with new ideas. Innovation is what social action is all about. If a standard solution was available for the problem, people would have applied it a long time ago.

Do take care of yourself. Celebrate the little victories, don't just wait for the big one. Take the time to keep a journal and process what is going on. Build a corner for reflection into every day. Burned out bodies are not the kind of advertisement that invites others to participate. An ounce of infectious energy is worth a pound of pedantic pushing.

The Art of Story-Telling

When we arrived in Termine, we were told by everyone — by each new person we met, and each person we encountered if we had not seen them for several hours — that "L'aria é buono, ma paese é brutto." Over and over, a ritual that ran through our heads and haunted us in our dreams: "The air is beautiful, but the village is ugly." That was their story, and they rehearsed it often enough to know it waking or sleeping. The air was good — 1,000 meters up in the mountains, crisp and clear; windswept clean. But the village?

When we first arrived, we saw only the quaint arches of rural Italian architecture. The walls were pictures of strength and craftsmanship, each stone carefully fitted into place and embedded in mortar. Clusters of houses dotted the hillside, their arches and angled corners making each a masterpiece of originality. The village was beautiful! The people were beautiful too. Not much education, but great wisdom. Hard working, dedicated to the land, generous.

Behind the walls, however, two out of three houses lay empty, mortar crumbling, woodwork rotting. Behind the walls, disheartened people. The village was dying, everyone knew it. Even Francesco, an elderly man who in many ways embodied a spirit of optimism, made sure we were clear. "The air is beautiful, but the village is ugly."

We started telling a different story. Houses could be repaired. We repaired the one we were living in as an example. A dairy farmer from the United States spent a week talking over fences the way only farmers can. Before the month was out, the first milking machine had been purchased and was in operation. A different story began to take form, ever so slowly.

I remember the day clearly, it was so significant. We had been in Termine about a year. Bright sun was streaming into the narrow lower street. Flora was out sweeping the piazza in front of her house. I had just come out of the social centre across from the church.

I met Francesco on the street. We stopped, talked about the village, about the cooperative, I forget what else. As I was about to go on my way, he said to me, "You know, the air is beautiful, and so is this village." We could have gone home right then, because the story had changed, and that meant the destiny of the village was to live.

Above everything else, Jesus was a story-teller. Need we say more?

Chapter 14

The Art of Loyalty

We have come out of the time when obedience, the acceptance of discipline, intelligent courage and resolution were most important, into that more difficult time when it is a person's duty to understand the world rather than simply fight for it.

— Ernest Hemingway[1]

In Thornton Wilder's play *Skin of our Teeth*, Mr. and Mrs. Antrobus are having marital difficulties. A young woman named Sabrina has been receiving far too much attention from Mr. Antrobus. Mrs. Antrobus reminds her husband of the promise they made to each other. Loyalty to that promise — not necessarily to each other — is what gives a marriage strength and endurance.

Loyalty to the Covenant

The Hebrew people were unique in that they thought of themselves as having a covenant with Yahweh, their God. They promised to be faithful to Yahweh. Yahweh promised to be faithful to them. In an era when there were many competing gods, a different god for just about every location, the Hebrews promised to be loyal to Yahweh as their God wherever they were. Yahweh promised to be with the people and to be their God, wherever they were. That was the covenant, as simple as that.

I think of my mother, being there for me when I was sick as a child, and my wife being there for me now when the flu is making my life miserable. Often you just need time to heal, but someone being there helps.

I think of my friends gathering around for my 50th birthday. One re-enacted my birth, complete with leaping nude from under the blanket that served as a womb. My 60th birthday was celebrated with a wine-tasting party given by friends who know I enjoy making wine. Having friends there for me was very important.

There is an art to being there for friends, and there is an art to being there with God. Some of us are visual and see God behind the beauty of a sunset, in the symmetry of a leaf or the smile of a friend. Some relate more through hearing, and know God in the rustle of leaves, the sound of a waterfall, the silence of the still night, the giggle of a baby. Others relate to their environment first through touch and texture. To them God mingles in the warmth of friendly surroundings, the feeling of peace that comes at the end of a day, the hug of a special friend. In the beginning, we are likely to experience God in only one of these ways. The art is to push beyond our primary mode of knowing and develop an awareness of God's presence through all three modes of perception.

The Circle Widens

Being there for God has its implications. If I am in covenant with God, and you are in covenant with God, then we have a responsibility to be there for each other. We need to care for one another because God cares for us all.

Moses knew what that was about. When you look at the Ten Commandments (Ex 20:1-17), three are about honouring God, one about caring for oneself, and six about care for our neighbour. In Christianity, this idea came to full bloom. Paul found a world ready for the one God who was there for everyone — Greek and Roman as much as Hebrew.

In the movie *Being There*, Peter Sellers plays Chauncy Gardner, a simple man with a mental handicap. When his benefactor dies, he walks out into a world he is totally unprepared to face. He is a man with no past, a person with no thought for the future, but someone who is totally there in the present. As events unfold we cannot help but admire this uncanny ability to be there for the one he is with. It wins him the loyalty of one person after another: the wife of a wealthy industrialist, the wealthy industrialist himself, the industrialist's friends, and eventually the king-makers looking for the next president of the United States.

At our baptism we made promises, or our parents made promises on our behalf, that we confirmed at our "confirmation." The words differ from denomination to denomination, but in one example they go like this:

- Do you believe that God has been made known to us in Jesus of Nazareth, who lived and died and lives again?
Yes I do.
- Do you believe that God by the Spirit is active in the world to direct and strengthen you?
Yes I do.
- Will you participate in the life of this congregation, supporting your fellow members with your presence and your prayers, and exercising those ministries to which God calls you?
Yes **I will.**

At this point the congregation enters the covenant as they respond to the question:
- Do you, the congregation of this church, receive these persons?
Yes, we do. We promise to welcome them into our fellowship, support them with our prayers, and challenge them to carry out those ministries to which God calls them.

For the Hebrew people and for Yahweh, loyalty to the covenant meant being there for each other. Baptism and confirmation celebrate a covenant between God, the congregation, sometimes parents, and the individual — a promise that each will be there for the other.

I do a fair bit of consulting with congregations in trouble. Nothing seems to be quite as explosive as clergy who show favouritism and minister to only one segment of the congregation. Sometimes it is because one group likes his or her ideas and another opposes them. Sometimes it is just personal chemistry. Whatever the circumstances, it is important for anyone in ministry to "be there" for everyone in the congregation. No exceptions. Because that's the way God is, just there for everyone — no exceptions.

Loyalty to the Mission

While going to Royal Military College, I spent my summers training with the Signal Corps. One day, our task was to practice creeping up on an enemy position until we were close, then rise and charge the last few feet. Several of us were assigned to be the enemy post. The weather was warm, the grass scented. We waited, and waited, and waited. A smoke grenade exploded. We went on the alert, expecting the attack at any moment. One lone figure came charging through the tall grass, shouting fiercely, supposedly facing six rifles and a machine gun post. Then he noticed none of his platoon were with him. We saw his courage evaporate, and a very sheepish lieutenant-in-training slunk back to find his troops. We found out later the smoke grenade had started a grass fire and the rest of the troop were busy putting it out, something their commander didn't notice when he gave the order to charge. He got the nickname "Combat" that day, and it stayed with him as long as I knew him.

Loyalty to the mission means the troops stay with their commander. Loyalty to the mission also means the commander keeps in touch with the real situation and with the troops. Sometimes in the church we charge this way and that, and moan because so few people follow us. The real situation is that over 50 percent of Canadians have no real relationship with a church or religious faith. They may carry health insurance and have access to hospitals, but have little or no idea of how to tap the resources of the church when they have a spiritual need.

Loyalty to the mission means keeping an eye on the goal. The mission of a hospital is not to maintain buildings but to provide a place where people can be treated for illness. The mission of a congregation is to provide spiritual care. Mission first means eye on the ball, not on the stadium.

Loyalty to the Truth

Many of us have found our faith changing as new ways of thinking challenge old theological understandings. The belief in the existence of heaven has disappeared for significant numbers of Christians over the last few decades, yet there has been great hesitation to raise the issue. "Why worry old Mrs. Jones," has been one rationalization. The wish to avoid conflict and protect salaries has been another. The result has been a growing separation between the church leadership and church members that is showing up in all kinds of ways.

The work of the Jesus Seminar has provided an occasion for bringing the results of contemporary biblical scholarship into the congregation. Marcus Borg's books are particularly helpful. The growing quest for spiritual depth is another avenue. The excitement of theological development, spiritual understanding and insights into the Bible is too good to keep from people. Truth, as they say, is stranger than fiction. It is the church's greatest asset in an age of increasing secularism.

Loyalty to Colleagues

We have not been very good at team ministry in the past. Many congregations called two clergy as a team, only to have conflicts erupt and disagreements send one or both packing. That record is improving, and we are now talking about professional ministry and lay leadership operating as a team. That makes team work doubly important.

There is only one secret to being a team — loyalty to your partner. That means working to ensure the other succeeds. If one team member fails, the whole team fails. When a team member is a success, the team is a success. In practical terms, this means sharing in the planning, assigning responsibilities, being there for one another as backup, and celebrating the victories.

Loyalty to Oneself

Recent surveys have shown an increasing number of professional clergy and lay leaders operating under a high level of stress. I feel stress when I'm doing something that is new or difficult. I feel very comfortable doing something where I have skills and enthusiasm. Jobs that are draining produce stress. Tasks that are energizing make me tired, but also make me spring out of bed with a feeling of excitement and anticipation the next day.

I think that is what Moses had in mind when he challenged the Israelites to move ahead into Palestine rather than remain wandering in the Sinai desert where they had already spent 40 years. His rallying cry for remembering obedience to God was put this way: "I set before you life or death, blessing or curse. Choose life, then, so that you and your descendants may live." (Deut 30:19)

To mature ministry into an art means discovering one's God-given gifts, developing those gifts and watching with excitement as they unfold. Loyalty in ministry means being faithful to those gifts and going with them as far as they will take you.

---

1   Quoted in William Bridges, *Managing Transitions* (Reading, Mass.: Addison-Wesley, 1991), p. 22.

Chapter 15

The Art of Staying in Love with God

We are shaped and fashioned by what we love.

— Goethe

Remember the first time you fell in love really hard? The world suddenly took on new colour. The days were not long enough to contain all the happiness. You felt invincible. You were not quite sure whether you were the centre of the universe, or the one you loved was the centre of the universe, but it had to be one or the other.

Do you remember the first time you fell in love with God? For me, the occasion was a summer church camp between first and second year university. There were about a hundred of us and the singing was marvelous. The days started with a talk in the outdoor chapel overlooking the lake. It finished with a campfire and starlight groups where we could share our deepest thoughts. The distant God I had admired from afar became a very close and accepting presence. I was in love.

Karl Rahner, a German Catholic theologian, defines faith as the handing over of oneself to ultimate mystery. Bernard Lonergan, a Canadian, describes it as "falling in love unrestrictedly." For me, there was an element of both in the experience. I have discovered that when one truly falls in love with God, or a person, there are no conditions, even if there remains a great deal that is unknown about the object of affection. For American theologian Paul Tillich, an encounter with God (he calls it the experience of grace) requires only one response, the courage to "accept the fact that we are accepted."[1] There was a strong element of courage involved for me as well.

The God one falls in love with and who loves back is not the unmovable, unchangeable potentate of medieval Christianity. Carter Heyward reminds us that love is a two-way exchange:

> If God loves us, the human-divine relation is reciprocal,
> dynamic, and of benefit to both parties. No lover is com-
> pletely autonomous, wholly untouched, finally unmoved
> by the loved one.[2]

A theology of love implies that just as we are changed by God's love, so God is affected by our love.

With time, a human love relationship deepens. A young woman named Mary sat in front of me in Grade 11 Math class. I asked her out to a movie, then to a dance. Before long we were "going steady," the regular date once a week with the occasional phone call in between. Then touching base every day became important. There followed engagement, marriage, deciding it was time to have children.

The same deepening characterizes our love relationship with God. It can begin in any number of ways. It usually results in attending worship more regularly. The relationship deepens as we read the Bible, participate in a prayer group, serve on a church committee, seek out ways to be of service to others. Those who continue the journey become more and more conscious of God's presence until all of life becomes a walk with God.

As with any human relationship, the romance with God can flounder. Spanish mystic, John of the Cross, called that development the "dark night of the soul." God seems distant. Worship is ho-hum. Prayer feels like a monologue. What do we do then?

At some point in every relationship there is the recognition that the flickering flame of love has become buried under the myriad details of daily life. The sense of romance that made life such an exciting journey of discovery all but disappears. That's the time to bring out the candles, make time periodically for dinner out, plan a weekend away. One way to counteract the busyness of life is by keeping a certain time sacrosanct for a daily check-in. I also find that as one gets older, the body responds more slowly. Taking the time for love-making to be an ecstatic event becomes increasingly important.

Many of these same techniques can be developed to keep the romance with God alive and well. But first a caution.

Falling in Love with Love

Remember the song, "Falling in love with love is falling for make-believe"? The feeling of being in love is very seductive, a warm, wonderful sense of being accepted that is at the same time liberating and energizing. When we fall in love, we want to find out everything about the other person. When we fall in love with love, the other is secondary to our exploitation of the sensation of being in love.

Infatuation is the name we give to falling in love with our first impression of another person. When we get around to discovering the person as they truly are, the reality can turn out to be very different from our dream. At that point the relationship can end, or deepen into a real love of the person as they actually are. What does it mean to get past an initial infatuation with God, to being in love with the God who is truly God?

We know people in three ways. We know others initially as objects we observe. We observe the way they dress, their actions, their responses to different situations. Even when people describe to us how they feel or what they think about something, we can receive that on one level with a dispassionate objectivity.

We can begin to interact on a deeper level also — as human beings. Will Herberg, an American Jewish scholar, used the term "dramatic knowing" to describe how the actions and words of another person resonate with who we are as a person. An illustration is the inner sense of what an actor or actress is going to do in a scene because we can imagine what we would do in the same situation.

A third way of knowing a person is through story-telling. While gathering information for his book *In Search of Excellence*, Tom Peters had a first hand experience of the power of story. "Two Hewlett-Packard engineers in their mid-twenties recently regaled us with an hour's worth of 'Bill and Dave' (Hewlett and Packard) stories. We were subsequently astonished to find that neither had seen, let alone talked to, the founders."[3] Story-telling can give a real feeling of knowing someone.

We learn a great deal about God through the stories others tell. The Bible is one collection of stories. Christian tradition and the religious literature of other faiths abound with many more. Likewise, we have within ourselves a dramatic identification with God. We sense God at work in creation, in others, and at work in the flow of history. Through the facility of "dramatic knowing" we resonate with what we see and identify God's activity underlying the beauty of creation and the actions of others. It is not that God has a "human" nature, but that whatever God is includes an aspect we can relate to as being deeply human.

It is easy to fall in love with the God of beautiful sunsets. But nature also includes mosquitoes and tornadoes. It is easy to like the God who comforts us through the smile of a friend, harder to accept the God who goads us into action through the harsh reproof of a colleague. Confining God within a romantic fantasy of our own making is an invitation to disillusionment and spiritual divorce, if not disaster.

So much for the temptation of falling in love with love. What does it mean to sustain a real love affair with God, as God truly is?

Spending Time with God

When we are in love, we want to spend more and more time with that person. The same is true of our relationship with God.

Some find silence a time when the presence of God is particularly near. I find a natural silence is important, and have difficulty with the contrived silence of some worship services that is interrupted by coughs and pennies dropping on the floor and planes flying overhead. Mall music as a cover-up does not improve the situation. Silence is, however, something very personal. You have to find your own quality of silence — the silence that is inhabited with the presence of God for you. It might be the silence of the drive to church or the silence of a walk early Sunday morning. It could be the silence during worship as the bread and wine are lifted in thankful anticipation.

I have found God in the words of a woman who shared her search for God. I have glimpsed God shining through a scripture read with passion. I have experienced God in the pageantry of an opening procession — a "parade" if you will — that said something important is about to happen, that we are entering a new space, that we can anticipate a new presence.

If you are a leader conducting a service, finding the presence of God may be more difficult in the midst of the business of contexting hymns and orchestrating participation. One congregation that I served had a wonderful organist and a dedicated choir. There was no need to worry about their performance, and the time while they were singing was a moment when I could often sense a caring Spirit presence.

I also found the presence of God to be very near when as a worship leader I could be completely myself in a service. That is not always possible, because it is important to provide a worship experience for a whole range of people, some of whom have personality traits and needs that are very different from our own. Something that works well for me is to do the so-called "pastoral prayer" sitting on a chair in the middle of the congregation. It is a matter of letting the congregation eavesdrop as I talk to my God who is both friend and counselor, who is my lover, yes, but also one whose love overflows the banks of personality and focuses my care on the needs of the world.

What is the overall effect of worship being truly a "date with God"? Celia Hahn of the Alban Institute describes what she has discovered people want from worship:

> People say they want to be warmly welcomed into a
> religious community where love is not only preached
> about but experienced, and then sent back out again with a
> sense of meaning that can undergird their everyday life.
> They want to return to work on Monday morning with
> their courage, caring, and integrity renewed.[4]

Bruce Reed identified the importance of a time of "extra-dependence" when someone else is in charge. Known as the "Grubb Theory of Oscillation," he found the deeper you oscillate into extra-dependence during worship, the more effective you are as a self-directed "intra-dependent" person the rest of the week.[5] Sensing the presence of God, and realizing God is ultimately in charge of our lives, can create the deepest relaxation, and consequently the most energizing renewal. That is one very real benefit of the power of keeping the romance alive.

The other benefit is that of spending time with someone you really love, an energizing, liberating "feel-good" experience if ever there was one.

That Special Place

A very special place for me is our family retreat centre in the midst of 80 acres of woods. One of the first things we did was to clear a path that we shortly dubbed "the cloister walk." Every monastery has an inner courtyard surrounded by a covered walk where the monks can stroll while reading their breviary or meditating. That's what our cloister walk has become for us, a pathway through God's nature where every step reminds us of the wonder of this world and the even greater wonder who is the Spirit that brought it all into being.

What is your special place? It could be a stone by a river where you can sit and think, or a bench in a neighbourhood park, or a favourite chair in the living room. Wherever it is, it is a place where God is near because it is a place where other concerns can be put on hold for the time being.

Some homes have a family altar. A simple cross on top of my dresser reminds me of God's presence.

Love Letters

You may still have a sheaf of love letters tucked away with your memorabilia, perhaps tied together with a ribbon. I know I do. What about love letters to God?

You can write a love note to God and pin it on the fridge: "Dear God; I love you because…"

A love letter that is more formal is a creed. Here are some lines from a creed that my wife Mary wrote 30 years ago:

> I believe in one god
> the most mature parent
> of all time who wasn't afraid
> to let a son walk
> down a dark street
> because he was given good reflexes. ...

> Society needs more lovers
> not lecturers.
> Faith is the oil on the body of a swan
> You can't see it but I'd like to see
> you swim without it.[6]

Faith continues to grow as love matures. Mary and I have been working on a creed that would describe what we believe today. It begins ...

> We believe there is a Spirit present everywhere that wills for the creative, for growth, for the evolution of a caring conscious society. We believe that each human being is loved, that the Spirit works for the well-being of each of us, irrespective of our colour, creed, station in life, physical or mental limitations, or sexual orientation. We believe that our role is to align ourselves with the creative energy of that Spiritual presence. ...

> We know this Spirit through the wonder that arouses our mind to a sense of awe, through the passion for life, and through the ecstasy that takes us outside ourselves into a sense of identity with others and the universe.

> As disciples of the Spirit we are called to reach out in love to others, to play a creative role in the development of society, to oppose injustice and foster the well-being of our neighbours.

> It is this Spirit that we call God.

Pushing the Edges

Every once in a while, extraordinary measures are required to bring romance back into life. We need to get away, do something completely different, break the daily pattern.

One ancient practice that can change one's daily routine very quickly is the fast. If you have any questions about your dependence or preoccupation with food, try doing without it for a time. There are health concerns, of course, and one should not enter any prolonged change of diet if that would place undue stress on the body. One form of fasting that we use every Easter is to restrict ourselves to juice and soup for the days of Holy Week, breaking our fast on Maundy Thursday with a meal that celebrates the Seder supper Jesus shared his disciples. It is surprising how much time is saved in the average day by not having to prepare meals or wash all those dishes. We use the extra time to read one of the books of the Bible, which can be a feast in itself.

There are a number of centres that offer silent retreats. The Jesuits are masters at this, and generally provide a spiritual director to guide your journey, someone who can suggest helpful spiritual exercises and give feedback on how you are doing.[7] There is something incredibly freeing about not having to make conversation with everyone you meet. People are all around you, there is companionship, but in the silence God becomes a closer companion, a partner as you spend time with scripture passages or walk outdoors.

Every male Moslem is obligated to make a pilgrimage to Mecca at one point during his life. By all accounts, it is a stirring event. Many Christians have found a trip to Palestine has enriched their relationship with God. Others visit Italy. One cannot be exposed to the spirit of St. Francis in Assisi, the religious art of Florence, the Benedictine heritage at Monte Casino, or the magnificence of St. Peter's in Rome, without being deeply affected.

The most profound way to show one's love for God, however, is simply by passing that love on to others. During an interview for the television series completed shortly before his death, Joseph Campbell, the master of mythology, told this story:

> A troubled woman came to the Indian saint and sage
> Ramakrishna, saying, "O Master, I do not find that I love
> God." And he asked, "Is there nothing, then, that you
> love?" To this she answered, "My little nephew." And he
> said to her, "There is your love and service to God, in your
> love and service to that child."

Joseph Campbell went on to add: "This is the high message of religion: 'Inasmuch as ye have done it unto one of the least of these...'"[8]

Those of us who minister in God's name want to be a channel for God's love to touch others. It is not hard to detect someone who ministers out of loyalty rather than love, out of duty rather than gratitude. The art of staying in love with God is important, for no other reason than that we are, as Goethe noted, "shaped and fashioned by what we love."[9] It is a good day if I can close it with the prayer, "Thank you, God, for using today to shape me a little more like your love."

1   See Paul Tillich's sermon, "You are Accepted" in his book *The Shaking of the Foundations* (New York: Scribner's, 1948).

2   Carter Heyward, *The Redemption of God* (Landan, Maryland: University Press of America, 1982), p. 6.

3   Thomas Peters and Robert Waterman Jr., *In Search of Excellence* (New York: Harper & Row, 1982), p. 75.

4   Celia Hahn, "Empowering the Saints Through Shared Ministry," *Action In formation* (May/June, 1987), p. 1.

5   Bruce Reed, "The Task of the Church and the Role of its Members," *Publi cation AL8* (Washington: The Alban Institute, ca. 1986).

6   Mary Woodbury, "god in small letters," *The Christian Century* (1964).

7   Loyola House in Guelph, Ontario, is one centre offering silent retreats dur ing certain weeks.

8   Joseph Campbell, *The Power of Myth* (New York: Doubleday, 1988), p. xvii.

9   Johann Wolfgang von Goethe (1749-1832).

A Final Word from both Authors

The Word of God is as fresh and lively, as full of change, as is the best of art and the most challenging of historical movements.

— Tom Driver[1]

You are God's extravagant art, God's extravagant generous work.

— Richard Caemmerer[2]

Religion has much to gain from art, just as art has much to gain from religion. The reason is that both religion and art receive their energy from their vision of the mystery underlying all creation. The arts experience the mystery of life and try to describe it through visual media or with sound. Religion experiences the mystery in life and tries to give structure to that experience, tries to capture and perpetuate the wonder of those moments when we feel closest to God. Both religion and art give life meaning by relating our individual lives to the mystery that lies at the heart of all life.

We believe that God's Word to us comes fresh with each new generation, each new experience, each new turning. That means it has to be continually communicated in a fresh way, a captivating way — that means through an art.

Richard Caemmerer, consummate artist and thinker, points out that we ourselves are a work of art, and uses the word *extravagant* to describe our incredible complexity. We believe that we are a work of art, challenged to use whatever art forms are most suitable to speak for our creator God, the ultimate artist.

Throughout history there has been a strong link between those with artistic vision and those with religious vision. Primitive tribes depended on their artists and artisans to create the totems, masks, rituals and dances that

159

enabled them to interact with the mystery of life. Renaissance artists sought to portray the depths of the inner life as well as the beauty and power of external form. Michelangelo saw the mystery in the human body and portrayed it in a way that not only attracted admiration but inspired reverence.

The advent of Protestantism brought about a separation between religion and the arts. The Anabaptists associated art with Roman Catholic worship and banned both from their churches. North American Puritans carried this tradition to an extreme with their white-painted meeting houses. Scottish Presbyterians refused to sing any hymns except the psalms set to music. One of the messages the Protestant church continued to give people until very recently was that art was a distraction, rather than an aid to the worship of God. In many main-line churches we try to confine art inside the frames of stained glass windows or within the practiced harmonies of choral anthems.

We admit that TV evangelists and the excesses of the charismatic movement have given passion a suspect if not a bad name. Yet passion is the soul of art, because passion supplies the energy for human endeavour.

We have proposed bringing passion in the form of our personhood into every one of our ministries until each becomes truly an art. Perhaps then we can go on to bring more of the traditional arts into our religious lives — modern painting, modern music, modern theatre, modern dance. That would make it a two-way street: we religious hearing what the arts have to say about the mystery; those in the arts hearing from a group of people who have specialized in being sensitive to the mystery we name God.

To make an art of a ministry means to be open to new and deeper insights into the nature of God and God's will for our times. It means being willing to incorporate those new understandings into our worship and our daily lives.

Finally, it means being willing to be passionate, to be moved — and to move others — emotionally. Art communicates ideas with an emotional power that moves hearts and changes lives. Jesus certainly did not lack passion, and a little more passion could well make our church one in which he would feel very much at home.

1   Tom F. Driver, *Patterns of Grace* (Lanham, Maryland: University Press of America, 1977), p. xxv.

2   Richard Caemmerer, St. Stephen's College Convocation Address, Edmonton, Alberta, September 28, 1988.

Also of interest from
The United Church Publishing House

The Man in the Scarlet Robe
Two Thousand Years of Searching for Jesus
by Michael McAteer and Michael Steinhauser

What do a veteran journalist and a New Testament scholar have in common? They are both fascinated by one of history's most influential figures — Jesus of Nazareth — and intrigued by the current popular interest in the mystery surrounding his personality. Who was Jesus Christ? What do we know about him? How has history, from the early Christian church to modern scholarship, viewed Jesus? Why does it matter for so many of us today? McAteer and Steinhauser join forces to offer us a comprehensive view of the current controversies surrounding the search for the historical Jesus, a search that began almost two thousand years ago and continues in our own time.

1-55134-042-9   **Paper $18.95**

God Hates Religion
How the Gospels Condemn False Religious Practice
by Christopher Levan

Is the church a colossal mistake? Has institutionalized religion corrupted the original intent of Christ's mission? Must the church "die" in order to make room for new life? With a powerful, prophetic voice, Levan declares that God has cause for concern, even disappointment, with the covenanted community. Many of us sense that our faith could be much more; that it is crippled by bureaucracy and tradition. Levan asserts that the church can break destructive patterns and be renewed — but only if it is willing to risk its own survival for the sake of an egalitarian community, patterned after the gospel's vision of God's coming reign on earth.

1-55134-045-3   **Paper $15.95**

Faith-full Stories
The Narrative Road to Religion
by John C. Hoffman

Stories are a crucial part of religious teaching, a pleasing way of conveying truth from one generation to another. Imagination and mystery, discovery and delight, are a part of seemingly simple stories that hold meaning for many of the world's peoples. In this challenging and insightful book, Hoffman offers intriguing evidence for that view and takes us further in his exploration of story types and functions from different faith traditions, regions, and eras. Hoffman guides us in determining a story's meaning and testing its truth — by listening to others tell *their* stories.

1-55134-008-9   **Paper $16.95**

Faithstyles in Congregations
Living Together in a Christian Community
by *Wilena G. Brown*

This volume provides an analysis of three faithstyles — community, searching, and partnership — found within all our congregations. Understanding the needs of each style can bring fruitful harmony and an appreciation of the gifts that each offers. A valuable aid for church leaders, outreach committee members, and all who engage in congregational life.

1-55134-006-2 Paper $12.95

Crosswalks
Prayers from a City Church
by *David R. Allen*

Drawn from over two decades of weekly public worship with an urban congregation, these poetic prayers are powerfully evocative and rich with imaginative insights. The prayers are organized by type — approach or eucharistic or thanksgiving — within the liturgical seasons of the church year and are suitable for private devotion and public worship.

1-55134-011-9 Paper $12.95

The Practice of Preaching
by *Paul Scott Wilson*

Wilson, professor of homiletics at Emmanuel College in the Toronto School of Theology, provides the definitive text on homiletics for theological students and practicing clergy. By synthesizing the four great historical traditions of rhetoric, hermeneutics, poetics, and oral presentation, Wilson presents a coherent and challenging vision of future homiletic directions. Dozens of written and oral exercises, definitions, sidebars, and sermon examples enhance the effectiveness and usefulness of the text. Wilson fosters a love of preaching and a love of language, and his work is deeply grounded in the history of preaching.

1-55134-035-6 Cloth $24.95 Canadian Rights Only

Leading Women
How Church Women Can Avoid Leadership Traps and Negotiate the Gender Maze
by *Carol E. Becker*

Carol Becker addresses the issues and concerns of the rapidly growing number of women in positions of church leadership, specifically how to communicate and influence decisions in a male world. She names the gender traps, examines the unique perspectives that women bring to leadership in the church, and explores communication strategies for women and men. Becker offers practical solutions for negotiating the gender maze for women working together with men in church leadership. Finally, she presents new paradigms for leadership to further the advancement of women in ministry.

1-55134-049-6 Paper $17.95 Canadian Rights Only